COOL
CARAVANNING

UPDATED SECOND EDITION

COOL CARAVANNING

A Selection of Stunning Sites in the English Countryside

Caroline Mills

IMM lifestyle books™

Read. Learn. Do What You Love.

Contents

Map/Cool for...		06
Introduction		08
Top Tips for Touring		10

North

1	Castlerigg Farm, Cumbria	12
2	Church Stile Farm, Cumbria	16
3	Borrowdale, Cumbria	20
4	Coniston Park Coppice, Cumbria	24
5	Lound House Farm, North Yorkshire	28
6	Sleningford Watermill, North Yorkshire	32
7	Howgill Lodge, North Yorkshire	36
8	Woodend Farm, North Yorkshire	40
9	Usha Gap, North Yorkshire	44
10	Finchale Abbey, County Durham	48
11	Highside Farm, County Durham	52
12	Kielder Village, Northumberland	56
13	Haltwhistle, Northumberland	60
14	Church Farm Organics, Merseyside	64

Midlands

15	Rowter Farm, Derbyshire	68
16	Bakewell, Derbyshire	72
17	Bank House Farm, Staffordshire	76
18	Oaklea, Lincolnshire	80
19	Fir Tree Farm, Warwickshire	84
20	Stratford Touring Park, Warwickshire	88
21	Monaughty Poeth, Shropshire	92
22	Whitcliffe Campsite, Shropshire	96
23	Rowlestone Court, Herefordshire	100
24	Hayles Fruit Farm, Gloucestershire	104

South-East

25 Sandringham, Norfolk 108

26 Willowcroft, Norfolk 112

27 The Dower House, Norfolk 116

28 The Orchard Campsite, Suffolk 120

29 Run Cottage, Suffolk 124

30 Waterclose Meadows, Cambridgeshire 128

31 Lincoln Farm Park, Oxfordshire 132

32 Hurley Riverside Park, Berkshire 136

33 Wellington Country Park, Berkshire 140

34 Chertsey, Surrey 144

35 Tanner Farm Park, Kent 148

36 Denny Wood, Hampshire 152

37 Chine Farm, Isle of Wight 156

South-West

38 Postern Hill, Wiltshire 160

39 Riverside Lakes, Dorset 164

40 Corfe Castle, Dorset 168

41 Burrowhayes Farm, Somerset 172

42 Alpine Grove Park, Somerset 176

43 Halse Farm, Somerset 179

44 Bolberry House Farm and Karrageen, Devon 182

45 Napps, Devon 186

46 North Morte Farm, Devon 190

47 Tristram, Cornwall 194

48 Beacon Cottage Farm, Cornwall 198

49 Treloan Coastal Holidays, Cornwall 202

50 Treveague Farm, Cornwall 206

51 Pentewan Sands, Cornwall 210

Index 214

Cool for...

LANDSCAPE LOVERS

The best sites for fabulous views

1   Castlerigg Farm
5   Lound House Farm
7   Howgill Lodge
8   Woodend Farm
9   Usha Gap
11 Highside Farm
15 Rowter Farm
16 Bakewell
19 Fir Tree Farm
21 Monaughty Poeth
22 Whitcliffe Campsite
23 Rowlestone Court
37 Chine Farm
44 Bolberry House Farm and Karrageen
46 North Morte Farm
45 Napps
49 Treloan Coastal Holidays
48 Beacon Cottage Farm
50 Treveague Farm

FIRST-TIMERS

For those new to the game

4   Coniston Park Coppice
20 Stratford Touring Park
25 Sandringham
27 The Dower House
29 Run Cottage Touring Park
30 Waterclose Meadows
31 Lincoln Farm Park
32 Hurley Riverside Park
35 Tanner Farm Park
41 Burrowhayes Farm
51 Pentewan Sands

KIDS

The top sites for families with young children

4   Coniston Park Coppice
6   Sleningford Watermill
14 Church Farm Organics
23 Rowlestone Court
27 The Dower House
28 The Orchard Campsite
31 Lincoln Farm Park
33 Wellington Country Park
35 Tanner Farm Park
39 Riverside Lakes
41 Burrowhayes Farm
45 Napps
47 Tristram
49 Treloan Coastal Holidays
51 Pentewan Sands

BEACHCOMBERS

If you are looking for sand, sea and surf

37 Chine Farm
45 Napps
46 North Morte Farm
47 Tristram
49 Treloan Coastal Holidays
48 Beacon Cottage Farm Touring Park
51 Pentewan Sands

TREE LOVERS

Sites in and around beautiful woodland

3   Borrowdale
4   Coniston Park Coppice
7   Howgill Lodge
13 Haltwhistle
18 Oaklea
25 Sandringham
27 The Dower House

33 Wellington Country Park
36 Denny Wood
38 Postern Hill
40 Corfe Castle
42 Alpine Grove Park

WATER BABIES

For those who love water, be it river, lake or coast

6   Sleningford Watermill
9   Usha Gap
10 Finchale Abbey
13 Haltwhistle
17 Bank House Park
19 Fir Tree Farm
21 Monaughty Poeth
26 Willowcroft
28 The Orchard Campsite
30 Waterclose Meadows
32 Hurley Riverside Park
34 Chertsey
37 Chine Farm
38 Riverside Lakes
47 Tristram
49 Treloan Coastal Holidays
51 Pentewan Sands

WALKERS

For those who like to put their best foot forward

2   Church Stile Farm
3   Borrowdale
4   Coniston Park Coppice
7   Howgill Lodge
8   Woodend Farm
9   Usha Gap
11 Highside Farm
15 Rowter Farm
16 Bakewell
17 Bank House Park
19 Fir Tree Farm
21 Monaughty Poeth

36 Denny Wood
40 Corfe Castle
41 Burrowhayes Farm
43 Halse Farm
44 Bolberry House Farm and Karrageen
46 North Morte Farm
47 Tristram
48 Beacon Cottage Farm

CITY FANS

For urban pleasures, try out these great sites

14 Church Farm Organics
20 Stratford Touring Park
22 Whitcliffe Campsite
31 Lincoln Farm Park
34 Chertsey

GOURMETS

Places to eat, drink and be merry

1   Castlerigg Farm
11 Highside Farm
14 Church Farm Organics
17 Bank House Park
23 Rowlestone Court
24 Hayles Fruit Farm
47 Tristram
50 Treveague Farm
51 Pentewan Sands

OUTWARD BOUND

The best sites for those who want action and adventure

6   Sleningford Watermill
12 Kielder
20 Stratford Touring Park
41 Burrowhayes Farm
47 Tristram
49 Treloan Coastal Holidays
51 Pentewan Sands

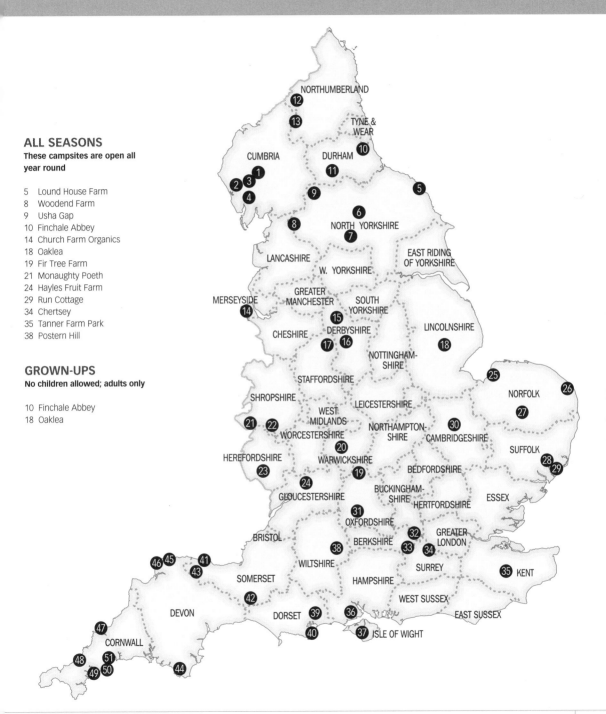

ALL SEASONS
These campsites are open all year round

5 Lound House Farm
8 Woodend Farm
9 Usha Gap
10 Finchale Abbey
14 Church Farm Organics
18 Oaklea
19 Fir Tree Farm
21 Monaughty Poeth
24 Hayles Fruit Farm
29 Run Cottage
34 Chertsey
35 Tanner Farm Park
38 Postern Hill

GROWN-UPS
No children allowed; adults only

10 Finchale Abbey
18 Oaklea

Introduction

Hello and welcome. Welcome to the updated second edition of *Cool Caravanning*, specifically for people who love to spend time in caravans or motorhomes, or at least use one as a base for exploration.

Most guides for caravanners – whether your 'van has an integrated engine or not – give a little bit of information about lots of campsites, often in symbol format, with maybe the odd picture, but nothing more. *Cool Caravanning* is different.

You might say *Cool Caravanning* is a movement, all about getting back to the fundamentals when selecting a campsite. So often the focus is on facilities; the accreditation system of stars, ticks or any other keyboard character used to grade campsites and caravan parks places more importance on the hairdryer and shaver points and other modern conveniences than on the location or the beauty of the site.

Cool Caravanning seeks to redress the balance and return to the reasons for why we go camping – location, location, location. Modern caravans and motorhomes tend to have every kind of luxury imaginable on board these days – complete wash rooms, kitchens and heating, with huge energy reserves and, often, solar-powered top-ups – so, all we really need from a campsite is a fresh water tap and waste disposal points. Most of the sites in this book have far more than that, though one or two don't. But what they all do have are fantastic locations without ugly uniform rows of 'vans, unless there's good reason.

If there is one thing we want when we go to a campsite, it's a great view or a superb place to stay. That's what camping is all about. It might be a panorama of the coastline, a view of the hills, a woodland setting or a pitch by a bubbling stream. It could be a site that allows things to happen, a city break, for example, or an opportunity to ride the waves. Each one of the sites included here has something special to offer.

But campsites are also about people. So often a campsite reflects the character of the owners; it is in many instances their home after all. And these sites represent that side of camping too. A great view of the hills can look terribly bleak if the welcome is frosty and unappealing. So, in the search to find a personal and hand-picked selection of the very best places to stay in England with a caravan or a motorhome, I've also looked at the background to a site – the ethos and the approaches to camping as viewed by the owners and wardens. Campsite owners are such a diverse bunch of people, from the youngest-at-heart to those with young families. What's apparent is it's cool to own a campsite – some have had long-held dreams of owning one.

Hundreds of campsites across the country were visited to make the selection for the first edition. One or two of the sites chosen have sadly closed down due to retirement or changed direction – they don't allow caravans or motorhomes any more! Most continue to thrive, evolve and get better with the passing years. But I've visited many more sites since the first edition was published. Very few would I have wished to include in the first guide in place of that original selection. Others are, indeed, wonderful, but there are not sufficient pages in a book to include them all. A first visit though, is always an attempt to establish whether the caravan park's website that says it 'nestles in the heart of …' really does, and whether, when they mention the sea view, they also forget to announce the roar of the motorway, the railway line that carries cargo all night long or the sea view that includes a nuclear power station – and there are some! If there is a downside to any of the campsites written about in *Cool Caravanning*, then I've not omitted to mention it, confident that the good points will far outweigh any niggles. And, because I consider myself to be extremely fortunate to live with my family in an incredible rural place, it takes quite a lot from a campsite location to really impress us enough to be somewhere we're prepared to pay to stay in our own 'van!

I make no apologies for being averse to TVs in 'vans. Travelling and holidays are all about getting away from the latest political troubles or the latest reality TV 'star' to fall victim to whichever knock-out programme they happen to be on. All caravans have giant picture windows and these sites are specially selected to make the most of them. And if it rains too much for the cagoule and boots, set out a board game and have some good old-fashioned family fun. So, for lovers of the great outdoors, or even for those who like to curl up on the sofa with a good book and a mug of cocoa while parked up in a nice spot, this book is for you.

There is such a diverse range of sites covered in *Cool Caravanning*, from tiny, almost exclusive, sites, such as Highside Farm (*see* page 52), to large sites like Pentewan Sands (*see* page 210), which, although bordering on a kind of commercial holiday park, still has something pretty special to offer. Most are independent sites, although a few are club-owned,

run by The Camping & Caravanning Club or The Caravan Club, but are open to non-members and don't have that cloned feeling that so many club sites can have. There are three small five-van certificated campsites as well, where only members of the relevant associated club can stay, but that feel so special they are worthy of obtaining club membership just to use them. And 25 per cent of the sites covered in the guide are open all year, so you can keep exploring through the winter months.

Each description provides details of the facilities, in brief, but also gives an insight into the whole of the campsite, the things to do and the places to go while staying, as well as useful information on special places to eat and drink or buy food, plus there's an alternative campsite should things get busy.

Above all, *Cool Caravanning* is about inspiration; to inspire you to pack up the caravan and spark a desire to visit one – or all – of these very special places, more often than not run by special people.

Happy travels – I hope you enjoy visiting these campsites and look forward to seeing you there.

Top Tips for Touring

WHAT TO EXPECT WHEN YOU ARRIVE AT A CAMPSITE

Hopefully a very warm welcome!

At medium-sized and larger touring parks plus club sites, you'll almost certainly find a short-term parking area in which to pull up with your motorhome or caravan while you check in. Make sure that you're not blocking the main entrance and exit. All of these parks will have a reception area, which may only be open at certain times of the day – in the morning for checking out and a couple of hours in the evening for checking in. If the reception is closed, there will be details of what to do – either a specific pitch will have been allocated for you, or you'll be advised to find a vacant pitch you like the look of so you can set up and return to check in later. Wardens live on site 24 hours a day on all club sites.

Small, certificated five-van sites are linked to a specific organization and, as such, you must be a member of the relevant club to stay. Often you'll be able to join upon arrival and, in any case, these are certainly sites that you make contact with prior to arrival. You may be asked for an estimated time of arrival to ensure that someone is around when you appear. But as these are generally people's homes, a quick knock at the door to say 'Hello' before you pitch up is courteous. That said, as many five-van sites are on farms, you may find the owners busy so, pitch up in the designated area and return to the front door later – or you'll find that the owner visits the site every evening.

At the very largest holiday parks (of which none are included in *Cool Caravanning*), where check-in may be on a specific day – with Saturday to Saturday bookings taken in peak season, for example – you may find check-in staff waiting on the approach road to direct you to the check-in area. Otherwise there will be a reception where you can check in and be provided with details of your pitch.

A 'VAN FOR ALL SEASONS'

There's no need to lock the door, shut the curtains and put your 'van into storage for the winter. With so many campsites open all year, take time to make the most of the chilly season with these top tips and advice for winter touring.

1. Check all water pipes for leaks; it's important to keep them above freezing to avoid costly damage. In below-freezing conditions, keep the waste drain tap open. If your 'van does not have Grade III classification (see opposite), where the water tanks will be insulated, a fish tank heater can be placed in fresh water tanks to prevent freezing. Make sure that you drain down both the fresh (including the water heater) and waste water systems and keep taps open when the 'van is not in use. If you're using an external waste-water tank with a caravan in really cold weather, it's worth purchasing an insulation blanket to prevent the contents from freezing. Keep a roll of 'Rescue Tape' (www.rescuetape.co.uk), used by the US military, in your 'van for emergency repairs to leaking pipes. It's self-fusing, and creates a permanent water- and air-tight seal around pipes.

2. Your 'van heater may have the option to use gas or electric power. Be very careful using additional electric heaters on site to keep your 'van warm; unless very low wattage, ideally they shouldn't be used at all. Check the rating of the campsite hook-up first, or you may find that you overload the circuit and leave fellow campers out in the cold!

3. Airing all soft furnishings in addition to bedding prior to a trip away will prevent them from feeling damp when you get into bed. Remember to keep some ventilation in your 'van during your stay or condensation will build, causing mould and damp upholstery/bedclothes.

4. Keep an eye on air vents to ensure they don't become blocked by fallen leaves or snow. Don't be tempted to cover up external vents; they're there for a purpose. It is possible to obtain a winter cover for fridge vents that aids performance in cold weather.

5. Add additional rugs and carpets to the floor for extra insulation and incorporate scatter cushions and throws into a living area to make it feel cosy. Keeping the blinds and curtains pulled during the day when it's not sunny will help to insulate the 'van and keep warmth in. Don't forget the roof blinds too.

6. Use products to keep the exterior of your van 'healthy' such as Fenwick's Overwintering Exterior, which will provide a protective wax coating and will protect your 'van from winter dirt.

7. Ensure that you're using propane gas rather than butane, which won't work below freezing – and make sure that you have a spare bottle ready to go with a quick changeover.

8. Keep a winter touring emergency kit with you so that you're fully prepared for poor road conditions or staying on site. A (plastic) shovel is essential but it should also include de-icer, an ice scraper and a brush. Carry

Grade III Classification

This is the highest industry standard for both insulation and heating. In addition to superb energy efficiency, it means that the water system will still work when the outside temperature is -15°C. Until recently, 'vans with Grade III classification have tended to be large coach-built motorhomes and premium-range caravans, but now many more mid-range caravans, motorhomes and campervan conversions have been awarded with the NCC EN 1646-1 Grade III classification for heating and thermal insulation.

Before any 'van can be granted its Grade III classification, the vehicle or unit has to be rigorously tested in a specially designed cold chamber facility, where it will be subjected to -15°C. The interior of the 'van must heat up to +20°C within four hours and be maintained at a stable temperature for a further hour. The water system must also work with a similar outside temperature. The test confirms that the 'vans are capable of maintaining a comfortable internal temperature for all-year-round touring, keeping owners warmer in winter and cooler in summer.

wheel grip mats (such as Milenco or Fiamma). They're useful to get traction started in slippery conditions – whether ice or a muddy field.

9. Make sure that you remove any snow build-up from the roof of your 'van before driving off. The police – or indeed other motorists – don't take too kindly to large amounts of the white stuff flying off while driving.

10. Towing a caravan is not recommended in icy or snowy conditions, but if it's absolutely essential that you do so, add something clearly visible to the front and rear. Being (generally) white, they tend to blend into the environment and can be hard to spot by other motorists. When driving a motorhome, reduce your speed considerably and increase your braking time. If your motorhome starts to skid, take your foot off the accelerator and brake, and gently steer in the direction you'd like to go. Only apply the brakes once you feel the vehicle regain traction. Alternatively, sit tight at your campsite and enjoy an extra few days' camping!

North

Castlerigg Farm
Cumbria

When the world was formed, someone must have sat on top of Castlerigg Fell and decided that this was the place from which to create a landscape. And when Doris Harrison selected a few fields of her farm for a campsite on the very same spot, it was a wise decision. Like some natural IMAX cinema, the views are 360 degrees – and you don't need 3D specs to appreciate them.

Doris's daughter Emma and her husband now run Castlerigg Farm Camping and Caravan Site. Tucked away along a no-through road, the only traffic past the site is to the farm next door, so there's no trouble with road noise at night. Nevertheless, civilization is close at hand for the seclusion-phobic, as Castlerigg Farm is just half a mile from the main road that cuts its way through the Cumbrian mountains and a couple of miles from the town of Keswick, which must boast more outdoor gear stores, as well as plenty of other shops, than any other English town.

Keswick can also boast of Bryson's, a traditional bakery where you can purchase tasty treats, such as Westmorland Fruit Cake and Lakeland Plum Bread. A few doors up the pedestrianized Main Street is Ye Olde Friars, a sweet shop that looks harmless enough with its timber-framed facade yet with contents that will make a dentist shudder. Amusements in the town vary from the unique Cumberland Pencil Museum, providing historical facts on the world's very first pencil, which was introduced in Cumbria, and modern pencil-making techniques, with a very good shop if you're into coloured pencils; and Theatre by the Lake – a regular regional winner in the UK Theatre Awards for the 'most welcoming theatre'.

Three miles east of the campsite is the Castlerigg Stone Circle, Cumberland's answer to Stonehenge; what it lacks in size, it makes up for with vistas.

Above: Caravans settled at Castlerigg Farm

From the campsite, when the road peters out, the public footpath begins, straight up the Walla Crag, the peculiarly named hill that climbs even higher than the one you've parked your 'van on and which has views that swallow up the whole of Derwentwater and Borrowdale beneath your feet. When darkness falls, the only light pollution is from the torches of campers in the tent field, which is separated by a stone wall, and a few twinklers from the village across the lake. It doesn't

---

Top Left: The impressive views from Castlerigg Farm **Bottom Left:** Cumbrian stone walls

matter how cold it may be, it's well worth turning out the lights in your 'van, parking your bottom on something comfortable outside and craning your neck skywards. Without the orange glow from cities lit with sodium, the stars are sure to draw your eyes upwards; and if they don't, the silhouettes of the fells west of Derwentwater as the sun sets behind, the final moment of the day lining each peak with a pink ribbon, certainly will. At daybreak the sun rises from Low Rigg on the other side of the campsite and you get a second chance to watch the natural magic show, the rising light turning the surrounding fields and fells into an iridescent jewel.

As you'll be unlikely to find a view of Derwentwater from your pitch, and if you can't face climbing Walla Crag for the jaw-dropping vistas, you should linger over your recycling and catch glimpses of the lake while doing your bit for the environment at the bin point.

There are plenty of hot-water showers, if you want to leave the Cumbrian mud in the country rather than treading it into your 'van, and a laundry for your hiking gear. Don't rely on the small site shop for creating a meal as it's basic (Booths supermarket is in Keswick), but the converted Hayloft Cafe (literally – it was once full of hay), within yards of the pitches, is a comfortable place for a bite to eat. Toasty in autumn, the log-burning stove is a welcoming focal point over which to enjoy breakfast or Cumberland sausage and sticky toffee pudding, and, as it's fully licensed, you can enjoy a drink knowing that you don't have to drive: perfect!

Designated a family/couples' site, there are no single-sex groups allowed, with rowdy behaviour discouraged; it is, after all, the echoes of the silent surrounding fells that are calling you to this campsite.

Castlerigg Farm Camping and Caravan Site

Keswick, Cumbria, CA12 4TE

01768 772479

www.castleriggfarm.com

info@castleriggfarm.com

Opening times: March to end of October

Facilities: Hot showers, hairdryers and shaver points in heated washroom, toilets, dishwashing room, laundry room with iron, payphone, small shop, battery charging, gas cylinder exchange, chemical toilet disposal point, hook-ups (though less electric points than pitches), dog exercise area and dog shower, gypsy caravan rental. Washing areas are kept immaculate.

How to get there: M6 junction 40, A66 to Keswick, A591 towards Windermere. One mile from Keswick (at top of the hill), turn right. Campsite is then a quarter of a mile farther on the left.

Food & drink: There's plenty of choice in nearby Keswick. The Wild Strawberry Coffee Shop is good for mid-morning and makes a good retreat from the outdoor gear shopping. And the smell of freshly sprinkled salt and vinegar is hard to resist from the open doors of The Old Keswickian, in the Market Square, serving great fish and chips, though not the cheapest.

Nearby attractions: Bassenthwaite is one of the lesser-known lakes to visit; glimpses can be seen from the campsite, while the wooded Thirlmere is also a short drive away. The towns of Penrith and Cockermouth, the latter with Wordsworth's family home, are equidistant from the campsite. Aira Force, a hurtling waterfall on National Trust land, provides an impressive walk.

Alternative campsite: Castlerigg Hall (www.castlerigghall.co.uk, tel.: 01768 774499). A few metres before Castlerigg Farm on the right. The site has a better aspect over the lake but, being lower down the hill and with terraced pitches, it doesn't have the 360-degree views that Castlerigg Farm has; otherwise, great facilities.

Top Left: Castlerigg Stone Circle
Top Right: Herdwick Sheep
Bottom: Panoramic view of Castlerigg Farm

Church Stile Farm
Cumbria

'I've never been camping in my life, I'm too soft,' said Mrs Knight, founder of Church Stile Farm Holiday Park. 'But I enjoy gardening and the environment and if I did go camping, I can imagine this is the kind of place I'd want to go to.' And so say all of us, for she created a space worthy of inclusion on any 'must visit' list, and deserving of its David Bellamy Gold Conservation Award. Julius and Kirsty Manduell now own and run the campsite and surrounding farm. They moved in during 2012, along with a flock of traditional Herdwick sheep. Thankfully, they've kept the campsite much as Mrs Knight created, with the exception of a few additions to improve it.

Above: The Screes Inn at Nether Wasdale

Of course, the views of the surrounding fells that you wake up to each morning help the atmosphere, with the Screes mountain range (yes, the one that plummets to the mysterious waters of England's deepest lake, Wastwater) within arm's reach of the campsite. And with Wastwater, once designated as 'Britain's Favourite View' by public vote, only 2 miles away, there's no denying that this is a fantastic location for a campsite.

Set in a woodland clearing, a narrow track rings a grassy area for motorhomes to pitch, some with hardstanding. Peppering the lawns are groups of shrubs, young trees – full of blossom in springtime, warming auburn leaves in autumn – and a mass of bulbs adding cheer to the gloomier of English days. Five static caravans, available to rent, are also on site, tucked away behind a beech hedge.

There's a large area of woodland within the campsite that shelters the pitches, with guided trails and the fabulous opportunity for little ones to make dens, collect acorns or act out all kinds of imaginative adventure stories. It also houses dozens of nest boxes for local tweeters. A public footpath connects up with the campsite, taking walkers to Wasdale, from where they can witness the most spectacular of views towards Wasdale Head, Great Gable and England's highest mountain, Scafell Pike. In fact, so iconic is the view that the National Parks authority uses it as its emblem.

The roads, enclosed with the finest of Cumbrian walls and local Herdwick sheep, are narrow around these parts, and with the road from Nether Wasdale to Wasdale Head a no-through road, it's recommended to use foot power for sightseeing, or at most a small car. Even the roads from Gosforth and Holmbrook are narrow, so take it gently. Thankfully, this area of the western lakes is less populated and far less tourist-orientated than the Windermere region of the National

Right: 'Britain's Favourite View': Wastwater

Park, so traffic is lighter. And, should you tire of the nation's favourite view, just turn around and look back from whence you came to see a green rolling landscape so utterly juxtaposed against the crashing crags.

When you enter the village of Nether Wasdale from Gosforth, two white-washed watering holes, one on either side of the road, greet you, the wide grass verges pulling the eye to the Screes mountain range in the not-so-far distance. Both establishments, The Screes Inn and The Strands Hotel, are inviting, with log fires for chilly days or gardens that must fall into the 'best pub view' category in warmer weather. The Strands Hotel, a CAMRA award-winning pub, has its own micro-brewery, so a fresh pint is always available. Both pubs are within staggering distance of the campsite, but if you feel the need to work up an appetite, make for The Bridge Inn on the edge of the River Irt in the neighbouring village of Santon Bridge – here you can listen to some tall tales, for it's the location of one of Britain's most unique annual competitions: 'The World's Biggest Liar'.

Once the blisters have all become too much, the feet begging for an alternative mode of transport, hop aboard 'La'al Ratty', the local name for the Ravenglass and Eskdale Railway, one village farther up the Eskdale Valley at Boot, and chug your way between the peaks. The steam train, which once transported iron ore from the mines, now operates an impressive 7-mile route that beats any commuter journey, and completes its travels at the quietly understated seaside town of Ravenglass.

Stretching along the coastline towards the mouth of the Solway Firth and the Scottish border, the Georgian town of Whitehaven offers an alternative view from the mountains. It has a fascinating history, with shipbuilding, coal exports and the trading of exotic goods all considered important industries at one time; it's little wonder there's plenty of spice in the local specialities.

Church Stile Farm Holiday Park

Nether Wasdale, Seascale, Cumbria, CA20 1ET

01946 726252

www.churchstile.com

Opening times: 1 March to 1 November

Facilities: 70 pitches, 24 hook-ups, clean and tidy amenity block with free showers, toilets, washbasins and family/disabled facilities, laundry room with iron, washing-up sinks, recycling bins, children's playground and ball area. Two glamping 'shepherd's huts'. Planning restrictions mean that motorhomes only can stay at this site.

How to get there: From A595 Barrow-in-Furness to Cockermouth road, turn off at Gosforth with signs for Wasdale. After 3 miles, turn right and drop down into Nether Wasdale; the site is on the left after the two inns and the church.

Food & drink: Both pubs in the village serve good, hearty dishes of local fare. For something really special, Low Wood Hall Country House Hotel and Restaurant sits on the hill above Nether Wasdale with great views over the village towards the Screes. Church Stile Farm also has its own farm shop and cafe.

Nearby attractions: Muncaster Castle, the beaches of the west coast, Ravenglass and Eskdale Railway.

Alternative campsite: Ravenglass Camping & Caravanning Club Site (www.campingandcaravanningclub.co.uk, tel.: 01229 717250). A quiet, tree-filled campsite next to open fields and within walking distance of the town and narrow-gauge railway.

Top Left: Parked motorhomes at Church Stile Farm
Bottom Left: A view over picturesque Wastwater
Right: Walking alongside Wastwater

Borrowdale
Cumbria

With names such as 'The Avenue', 'Cat Bells' and 'Lakeside Gardens', you'd be forgiven for thinking you were on the set of an American soap. These are, in fact, the enclaves from which to select a pitch at Borrowdale Caravan Club Site, where you can glimpse the south-western fringe of Derwentwater and Borrowdale.

Sited on land owned by the National Trust and managed by the Caravan Club (non-members are welcome), the campsite is hidden beneath a canopy of woodland, with four pitch enclosures separated by marshy areas teeming with wildlife, which are in themselves a major attraction. The wardens have put up nest boxes and bird feeders everywhere so guests can watch red squirrels and birds from the comfort of their 'vans – you can even buy bird food at the reception area.

Leave the television at home and on arrival turn off your mobile phone. You won't need the former and the neighbouring fells are unkind to signal reception for the latter. Instead, fling open the 'van door, don a stout pair of boots and take a deep gulp of fresh, lakeside air. Soporific, it's a great aid to a good night's sleep, as is the gentle sound of the trickling stream that cuts across the entrance to the site.

Low Manesty is a campsite that is enjoyed by the self-sufficient. While there are the basic requirements, such as freshwater taps, chemical toilet emptying points and waste disposal facilities, there are no ugly shower

blocks to blot the peaceful surroundings, so you need to use your own on-board resources or brave the chilly temperatures of Derwentwater and bathe alfresco.

Above: Birdwatching at Borrowdale

Beauty lies beyond the campsite, too, with the views of the fells and lake tantalizing through the tree trunks. There's some serious fell walking to be had within a few steps of the site entrance, where the climb of Black Crag begins. But there are less stenuous strolls, too, and these are even feasible with an off-road, three-wheeler pushchair when the family is in tow. Two footpaths from the site take you down to Lake Manesty Woods or Derwentwater, connecting up with public paths, lake views northwards or through fields around the southern tip to the nearby village of Grange. There are plenty of places to paddle along the lake shore and within 20 minutes walk of the campsite is the High

Left: Derwentwater

Brandelhow landing stage for the launch service around Derwentwater, undoubtedly one of the finest ways to travel. Alternatively, the Keswick–Buttermere bus stops right outside the site entrance.

For a fine walk with refreshment, follow the Cumbria Way that skirts the lakeside edge of the campsite to the village of Grange where you've a choice of eateries to warm the cockles and boost the energy levels. Grange Cafe has the better food and service but the Grange Bridge Cottage Tea Shop wins on location, for the tea garden overlooks the River Derwent and the double-humpback bridge that gives the tea room its name. For an upmarket evening meal, the Borrowdale Gates Hotel is within walking distance of the campsite.

The Borrowdale/Lorton Vale road is one great loop and, beyond Seatoller, the Honister Pass has a 1:4 gradient unsuitable for towing caravans – and even large motorhomes, unless you're really confident of your vehicle's braking system – so the only way to and from the site is via Keswick. The Caravan Club's recommended route is through the village of Grange, but go easy on the double-humpback bridge and watch for narrowing roads, as walkers often park their cars along the verge, making it mighty tight in places.

The campsite is a great base for exploring the northern lakes, such as the lesser-known Bassenthwaite or wooded Thirlmere, the poetically named Buttermere (with the remains of the District's most well-known walker, Alfred Wainwright, buried in the village of the same name), Cockermouth (the birthplace of poet William Wordsworth) or, a little farther east, Ullswater. There are also some gentle walks to be found along the eastern shores of Derwentwater, with off-road parking at various National Trust car parks along Borrowdale.

Borrowdale Caravan Club Site

Manesty, Keswick, Cumbria, CA12 5UG

01768 777275

www.caravanclub.co.uk

enquiries@caravanclub.co.uk

Opening times: April to beginning of November

Facilities: 60 hardstanding pitches with hook-up, motorhome service point with chemical toilet waste disposal and small shop (basics only, including gas). No sanitation block.

How to get there: Junction 40 on M6 at Penrith, A66 to Keswick, B5289 Borrowdale and Rosthwaite. Turn right at signpost for Grange. Take care over double humpback bridge and through village. Site on right in 1 mile.

Food & drink: Two tea rooms in the village of Grange, meals for non-residents at Borrowdale Gates Hotel close to campsite. More hotels and cafes in nearby Rosthwaite and Seatoller. Supermarkets in Keswick.

Nearby attractions: The hamlet of Seatoller, The Cumbria Way, Lodore Falls (good viewpoint), walking and cycling, Keswick.

Alternative Campsite: Seatoller Farm (www.seatollerfarm.co.uk, tel.: 01768 777232). A very basic site with no hook-ups or service points but a fantastic location. Tight turn.

Left: Walking alongside Derwentwater
Top Right: Woodland pitches at Borrowdale Caravan Club Site
Bottom Right: The village of Grange in Borrowdale

Coniston Park Coppice
Cumbria

On the map it's shaped like a long, bony finger pointing towards the lesser-known tarns and Langdale Valley, but the dark depths of Coniston Water stirs up other connotations – Donald Campbell's speed records in Bluebird and his resting place since 1967, before the recovery and burial of his body at Coniston village in 2001. Walking along the western shores of the lake, especially in early sunlight before the rest of the world treads the same path, one wonders if you can hear the roar of a jet engine, before realizing that the only noise is of water rustling where the lake meets land.

Above: Pitches at Park Coppice

Look east across the lake and the multicoloured expanse of Grizedale Forest catches the eye; turn west and the conical-shaped Old Man of Coniston casts a watchful glance over the lake. Often snow-capped for several months of the year, the Old Man bears a passing resemblance to an ash-covered volcano ready to spit the Lakeland's bowels onto the neighbouring fells.

In between the Old Man and the reflective waters sits the 63-acre wood that the Coniston Park Coppice campsite inhabits. Managed by the Caravan Club (non-members welcome), it's a large site even by global standards, with 252 hardstanding pitches for caravans and motorhomes, each with an electric hook-up. But big doesn't have to mean impersonal or featureless; with the trees providing a roof, shelter, backdrop and pitch dividers, the site has been thoughtfully landscaped with small clusters of pitches grouped in open glades, like modern cul-de-sacs, off two central roads. Each glade is named after one of the district's lakes, and all the pitches are pretty much level, with some dug back into the woodland banks, while the site slopes gently down towards Coniston Water. As would be expected from such a large site, there are plenty of facilities in terms of service points and amenity blocks housing toilets, hot showers, baby changing, laundry and dishwashing facilities. But man-made entertainment has been avoided with the exception of some outdoor play areas for the tinies. Barbecues are allowed, but open fires are not permitted.

Under the trees, the site is refreshingly unsanitized – a place for lovers of the great outdoors not afraid of mud or the odd acorn that, come autumn, decides to plop from the overhead branches, causing a mini explosion on the 'van roof. But the real boon for this site is its watery neighbour. There's direct access from the campsite to miles of lakeside paths that the smallest of feet can toddle along and the most determined of

Right: Coniston Water

experienced ramblers can enjoy. A mere 360 metres from the campsite is a launching point for canoes, windsurfers, rowing boats or dinghy sailing – a car park at the bottom of the campsite, close to the lake, is available for guests wishing to launch watercraft. Fishing is also possible with the right permission. And within a 1-mile lakeside walk is Coniston Pier, from where boats can be hired or a trip can be taken on the Steam Yacht *Gondola*, a beautifully restored Victorian lake cruiser that, between March and the end of October, glides a virtually silent path through the dark waters. Keeping up with environmentally conscious times, the *Gondola* no longer burns coal, opting for compressed waste-wood logs to power its steam engines.

A little farther on from Coniston Pier is the village of Coniston, a busy tourist magnet housing the Ruskin Museum, dedicated to the lives of three men – John Ruskin, Arthur Ransome and Donald Campbell – that have made a mark on the history of Coniston Water. On the eastern side of the lake, accessible by the *Gondola*, is Brantwood, the former home of art and social critic John Ruskin, with fabulous views over the lake and memories of writer Arthur Ransome, whose tales of adventures in *Swallows and Amazons* were partly based on Coniston Water.

And on the theme of literary giants, a few miles farther is William Wordsworth's house, Dove Cottage, and his final resting place in the family grave at Grasmere. The neighbouring Wordsworth Daffodil Garden, in tribute to his poetic classic, is worthy of a reflective visit, especially in spring when the yellow trumpets are in full bloom. Or you can return to your childhood with a visit to Hill Top, the snug home of Beatrix Potter at Near Sawrey. It's possible to sink a pint of the local in the Tower Bank Arms next door, too; you'll recognize the pub, if only subconsciously, for it features, with identical detail, in *The Tale of Jemima Puddleduck*.

Coniston Park Coppice Caravan Club Site

Coniston, Cumbria, LA21 8LA

01539 441555

www.caravanclub.co.uk

enquiries@caravanclub.co.uk

Opening times: Open all year

Facilities: 252 hardstanding pitches all with electric hook-up, three amenity blocks with hot showers, motorhome service point, laundry and baby-changing facilities, dishwashing area, recycling, play areas, shop including gas, public transport 400 yards from entrance. Dogs welcome.

How to get there: Junction 36 on M6 and A590 towards Barrow. At Greenodd, turn onto A5092, signpost Workington. In 2 miles fork right onto A5084 towards Coniston. At Torver, turn right onto A593. Site is on right in 1¼ miles.

Food & drink: Heritage Meats (www.heritagemeats.co.uk), based at Yew Tree Farm (once owned and lived in by Beatrix Potter) near Coniston, sells lamb and beef direct from the working hill farm, including local Herdwick sheep. It's ideal if you're looking to put something on a BBQ. For some of the best Cumberland sauce and a massive selection of other locally made condiments, head to the Hawkshead Relish Company in Hawkshead.

Nearby attractions: Coniston and Hawkshead offer plenty of tourist shopping and tea rooms. In Coniston the Ruskin Museum pays tribute to the lives of Arthur Ransome, Donald Campbell and John Ruskin, while in Hawkshead the Beatrix Potter Gallery shows a changing exhibition of original illustrations from the author's books. Grizedale Forest Park provides plenty of opportunity for gadding about in the fresh air.

Alternative campsite: Hawkshead Hall Campsite (www.hawksheadhall-campsite.co.uk, tel.: 01539 436221). A grass-only site with limited pitches for caravans/motorhomes, so booking is advisable.

Top Left: Woodland walks alongside Coniston Water
Bottom Left: Birdwatching in Park Coppice
Right: Boat launching close to the site

Lound House Farm
North Yorkshire

The very mention of the word 'moors' sounds bleak and, indeed, there are parts of the North York Moors remote enough to find yourself entirely alone, a factor that should hardly be discouraging to visitors in a country where it gets progressively harder to grab a moment of solitude. The uplands are a product of millions of years of geological reorganization; they were given the glacial treatment for a little while before melting ice sliced through the rock, forming deeply gouged valleys with contradictory streamlets and jagged escarpments around the edge.

A sea of heather provides the Moors with a thick blanket of colour to brighten up the last days of summer and lead us cheerfully into autumn before returning the moors to their mixed tones of browns and beige for winter, when the frost casts a shiny veil over the bell-shaped plants, encouraging walkers to leave the comfort of the fire and head out to explore.

And an enthusiasm for travel is something the Moors have inspired for generations. Captain James Cook, one of England's finest explorers, was a child of the North York Moors. His intrepid exploration and cartographic skills have put many a traveller's ambitions and hastily scribbled directions on the back of a beer mat to shame. There are monuments and museums all over the moors dedicated to him, although surely the best way to show appreciation to the man is to get out a map and explore for ourselves?

One of the best places from which to start any exploration is Lound House Farm. High on a hill, by a cluster of tiny villages on the edge of the Moors, it has sweeping views of Captain Cook's frequent departure point, Whitby, and the Saltwick Bay coastline that runs south of the town. The campsite is virtually circular, the pitches working their way round the central farmhouse – a traditional, sturdy Yorkshire building made from the weather-blackened blocks of stone

Above: Sea views from Lound House Farm

that are even stronger than a cup of Yorkshire tea. With a mixture of hardstanding and grass pitches, pretty much everyone gets a view of the sea, such is the curve of the coastline. And between the site and the cliffs lie field after field of green pastures and agricultural land with a small wood behind the site. It's certainly quiet, and the small road that runs past only

Left: Whitby, with St Mary's Church in the background

leads to a couple of tiny hamlets, so there's more chance of hearing the twice-yearly visit of the tractor to the neighbouring field than the road.

It is, however, the views that make the site, and it has a deliberate policy of keeping things simple. There is a toilet and fresh water, but that's about it. No showers, no play equipment (apart from the very best of rubber tyres tied to a tree and a large grass area for the imagination), no shop and no reception, other than the warm welcome that you'll receive from the Bainbridges upon arrival.

Once the tea has brewed and it's time to explore, take a trip up the coast road from Whitby to Staithes. It's a tiny fishing village where the houses cling to the steep cliffs of a ravine like limpets and the power of the sea is evident on the rocks and in the tales told by the residents. It's here that the boyish James Cook lived for a time, discovering his love of the sea before being let loose in Whitby. There's a great Heritage Centre in the village, where a treasure trove of bits and pieces associated with his life have been collected along with a replica of the shop where he once worked.

Before making the heart-pounding walk back up the hill (Staithes is so tightly compact around the harbour that visitors must park at the top of the hill by the entrance to the village), prepare for your short journey by quenching your thirst at one of the pubs close to the harbour. They're frequented by the village fishermen, so you may well hear tales of smuggling and stories, both tragic and heart-rending, of the sea and this close-knit community.

Lound House Farm

Littlebeck Lane, Whitby,

North Yorkshire, YO22 5HY

01947 810383

Opening times: Open all year (weather permitting)

Facilities: 35 pitches, hook-ups, toilets, cold-water taps, chemical toilet disposal point.

How to get there: Do not use SAT-NAV, rather follow this route in order to avoid steep hills and very narrow lanes. A171 to Whitby. In Whitby, turn onto B1416 signed for Ruswarp. Two miles past Ruswarp, turn right signed for Littlebeck. Site is half a mile farther on the right.

Food & drink: It has to be fresh Whitby fish and chips: Trenchers', opposite the railway station and harbour, are 'posh' fish and chips; Hadleys', over the bridge in the Old Town, are particularly fine. Quayside has previously won Fish and Chip Shop of the Year. For cooking in your own 'van you can buy fresh fish from Sandgate Seafoods, on Sandgate.

Nearby attractions: Whitby Abbey and St Mary's Church are landmarks in the town (and can be seen clearly from the campsite). Climb the famous steps to reach the abbey. Head to Goathland, one-time Aidensfield in *Heartbeat*, and set foot on the North Yorkshire Moors Steam Railway for a spectacular ride. For a geological wonder, visit the Hole of Horcum – a three-quarter-mile-wide crater and relic of the Ice Age – next to the A169.

Alternative campsite: Hooks House Farm (www.hookshousefarm.co.uk, tel.: 01947 880283). Lovely site with fantastic views of Robin Hood's Bay (some road noise).

Top Left: The picturesque town of Whitby
Bottom Left: Sea views from Lound House Farm
Right: Good old-fashioned fun at the farm

Sleningford Watermill
North Yorkshire

You don't have to be mad keen on canoeing to stay at Sleningford Watermill, but it helps. In fact, the chances are that even if you had no intention of performing a barrel roll in the water when you arrived, you'll at least be dipping a big toe in before you leave. And if you're not a canoeist of any kind (and by canoeist, I mean anyone from the age of 3 to 103 who might like to have a go even if they've never stepped foot in one before), be prepared for those who are, because the rainbow of canoes, kayaks, inflatable dinghies and anything else that floats is unmissable around the park.

Above: Canoeing on the River Ure at Sleningford Watermill

Like so many attractions, it's the lure of the water that draws people to Sleningford Watermill. In this instance it's the River Ure, which rises way back in the far west of the Yorkshire Dales and by the time it reaches the now defunct but beautiful watermill is wide enough and frothy enough to provide some serious entertainment. There's a long stretch directly in front of the campsite that appeals to canoeists of all abilities, as well as to fishermen throwing a fly. While there is a touch of torrential white water to attract hardened experience, just a matter of feet away is the polished calm of a water tamed, ready to accept young hopefuls and paddlers alike who just want to splash.

It is without doubt a fantastic campsite. Far away from the road, down a long private drive, the first pitches are raised above the entrance and are for seasonal touring caravans. They are, rather alarmingly at first, in a neat row, so that everyone gets a view of the river, but this is the only part of the site that's uniform. In the extensive centre of the park is the old watermill and a series of stone barns and stables that have been converted into changing rooms (for canoeists) and camping facilities, as well as the reception and shop. This is the hub of the site, busy with ice-cream eaters and campers going about their daily business. More pitches are set up on the grass directly in front of the river and the watermill. Known as 'The Riverside', it is the best place to pitch if you want to be in the centre of it all but not if you'd prefer some peace.

Behind the reception is 'The Millhouse Field', the quietest of the three campsite areas; totally enclosed

by hedges and trees; here you can find a peaceful corner as there is no through access. It tends to be the area totally given over to 'vans because every pitch has access to hook-ups. But by far the most picturesque and natural area of the site is 'The Island', a vast parkland meadow right next to the river where you can select a pitch with or without hook-up. Nothing is defined here – just choose a spot you happen to like, whether it's by the water's edge, under a giant oak tree or tucked up against the hedges. The meadow is brimming with wildlife and plants. In between the areas mown for campers to pitch and along parts of the riverbank, large swathes of grass are kept long, where wildflowers erupt and dragonflies dance. Secret paths weave their way beneath the wild shrubs and trees, trodden down by eager river-seekers.

It's here where many of the canoeists stay, as well as nature lovers, as it's furnished with bug hotels and hidey-holes for creatures and is where birds look for nests from which to rear their young. A small sandy beach, from where the intrepid enter the river, is overlooked by an eroding cliff on the other side that has more holes than a pack of Polo mints and is home to a colony of migrating birds. As the canoeists try to paddle upstream, fighting against the white water, the sand martins dart at full speed in and out of their makeshift nests, dipping and diving above the water as if to increase the pace of the activity below.

I happened to be on site at its busiest time of year and even then, when the giggles and resonating laughter of happy children fill the pure Yorkshire air, there were still quiet places to pitch and solitary spaces to hide oneself away, where you could close your eyes under a midday sun and soak up the sound of the river, oblivious to all but the breeze through the trees.

Sleningford Watermill

North Stainley, Ripon, North Yorkshire, HG4 3HQ

01765 635201

www.sleningfordwatermill.co.uk

sleningfordwatermill@gmail.com

Opening times: Beginning of April to end of October

Facilities: Three contrasting pitching areas, hook-ups, free hot showers, toilets, disabled facilities, laundry, dishwashing, recycling, shop selling local produce plus camping equipment, fly-fishing, canoe/kayak river access. Dogs on leads welcome.

How to get there: A1(M)/A1, come off at turning for B6267, signed Masham. Follow road for 3 miles, turn left, signed West Tanfield. In village, turn left onto A6108 and cross river bridge. Site is half a mile from West Tanfield on left.

Food & drink: The Staveley Arms (tel.: 01765 635439) in North Stainley has a good menu, local ales and is within walking distance of the campsite.

Nearby attractions: As well as canoeing and fishing on the river, head to the lovely village of Masham and visit one of two breweries, Theakston Brewery or the rival Black Sheep Brewery, set up by a Theakston family member.

Alternative campsite: The Black Swan (www.blackswanholiday.co.uk, tel.: 01765 689477). Good old-fashioned village pub in Fearby with a campsite at the rear and great views of the Dales. Six miles from Sleningford Watermill.

Top Left: Camping at Sleningford Watermill
Top Right: The old watermill
Bottom: The River Ure

Howgill Lodge
North Yorkshire

Choices, choices. The Yorkshire Dales National Park is brimming a-plenty with campsites of all shapes and sizes, and you're guaranteed a decent view almost wherever you stay. There's a goodly supply of campsites and caravan parks in Wharfedale alone, the National Park's most south-eastern dale.

So you can imagine the difficulty in selecting only one of Wharfedale's campsite collection. I've plumped for Howgill Lodge, at no detriment to the others (I'd happily recommend Masons at Appletreewick, Causeway Caravan Site at Kettlewell or Wood Nook near Threshfield). Why Howgill Lodge? Well you know you've arrived somewhere special when there's a lengthy trip along a near-private drive off the main road to reach the campsite, and chickens are roaming the grounds.

Of course, these alone don't make a great campsite. I expect a warm welcome and you'll certainly get that from the Foster family who have owned and run Howgill Lodge for many years. But you'll find plenty more to recommend it – the location first and foremost. Arrive in the dark, pull your curtains back in the morning and you'll understand what I mean.

The River Wharfe winds its way south and east from Oughtershaw Beck in Langstrothdale to flow into the River Ouse south of York. Howgill Lodge sits a handful of miles north of where the Wharfe exits the Yorkshire Dales National Park at Bolton Bridge. You have little for

Above: The garden atmosphere of Howgill Lodge

company other than your campsite neighbours – and it's bliss!

Sited at the western foot of Barden Fell, the campsite is terraced, with pitches making the most of views across Wharfedale to the bulk of Burnsall and Thorpe Fell. Should you wish to turn and look the other way, the crags of Barden Fell appeal and shelter at the same time. With only 20 pitches and tucked away along a tiny lane, the site never feels horrendously busy – it's as if you've found your own private hideaway that you just happen to be sharing. If you have a notable 'others' who don't camp, Fiona and Tony Foster can put them up in their B&B, converted from a rather lovely 17th-century barn.

Indeed, with the magnificent views, the terraces that slope down to the diminutive Fir Beck, the shrubs and colourful flowers and the chickens wandering the site, you feel as if you're pitched up in a private garden. And

Left: Views of the countryside from Howgill Lodge

the Foster family care for their garden and patch of North Yorkshire with a passion.

While the site is well kept, it's not clinical – the Fosters like to leave some areas uncut to encourage local wildlife, there are bird boxes about and the sewage system is an eco-friendly reed bed (hence you need to use formaldehyde-free toilet chemicals). Solar panels have been installed for lighting and to heat the water – and guests are encouraged to walk or use public transport to get around.

And that's not a problem, for Wharfedale is the most idyllic stomping ground. Within a five-minute walk from the campsite you'll find the River Wharfe and the Dales. You can walk to Grassington, just one of the numerous scenic villages within Wharfedale, and then catch the bus back – it stops at the end of Howgill Lane. But if it's understated, near-silent beauty that you're after, make a point of seeing Upper Wharfedale and Langstrothdale, through which the most northern stretch of the Wharfe trickles. It's a very special landscape, bursting with sheep-filled meadows and wild flowers.

South of Howgill Lodge is the 30,000-acre Bolton Abbey Estate. It's a popular tourist attraction, with the ruins of the Priory providing an atmospheric location for a wander, not forgetting a hop, skip and jump over the stepping stones across the Wharfe.

The nearby market towns of Skipton and Ilkley offer a good day out, with Skipton Castle, one of the most complete medieval castles in the country, delivering plenty of Yorkshire history to absorb. Of course, you can absorb plenty in Ilkley too – the fresh cake counter in Betty's being a good starting place! A Yorkshire institution, I'd recommend taking a bag of Betty's Yorkshire Fat Rascals back to the campsite to serve warm while enjoying the view across the dale.

Howgill Lodge

Barden, Skipton, North Yorkshire, BD23 6DJ

01756 720655

www.howgill-lodge.co.uk

info@howgill-lodge.co.uk

Opening times: End of March to end of October

Facilities: 20 hardstanding pitches with hook-up, toilets and hot showers, dishwashing, chemical toilet disposal point, fresh water, motorhome service point, well-stocked shop (including local sausages, bacon and milk, plus eggs from the campsite chickens), gas sales, wi-fi, recycling, B&B. Dogs welcome.

How to get there: From A59 Skipton to Blubberhouses road, turn left at Bolton Bridge onto the B6160 and into Lower Wharfedale. At Barden Tower, turn right over Barden Bridge and follow the road north as it becomes Stangs Lane. In just over a mile, turn right along Howgill Lane. Site entrance on left in ¼ mile.

Food & drink: The New Inn (www.the-new-inn-appletreewick. com, tel.: 01756 720252) and The Craven Arms (www.craven-cruckbarn.co.uk, tel.: 01756 720270) at Appletreewick, a 1-mile walk from Howgill Lodge. Both serve good food and cask ales and have fine views of Wharfedale.

Nearby attractions: Bolton Abbey, Skipton Castle and the Embsay & Bolton Abbey Steam Railway are the most obvious choices nearby. The town of Ilkley, with Betty's Tearooms, shouldn't be missed, but if you're a keen garden visitor neither should Parcevall Hall Gardens, near Appletreewick.

Alternative campsite: Masons Campsite (www.masons campsite.co.uk, tel.: 01756 720275) 1½ miles northeast of Howgill Lodge on the western outskirts of Appletreewick: flat, grass-field campsite on the banks of the River Wharfe. The site can get very busy with tents in summer.

Top: Summer in Wharfedale
Bottom Left: Grassington is a popular village to visit
Bottom Right: Terraced pitches at Howgill Lodge overlooking Wharfedale

Woodend Farm
North Yorkshire

Woodend Farm is the kind of campsite that, if you don't know about, you tend only to discover by chance. That's because It's not on the side of a busy main road and it's barely signposted. So, unless you've been past it before, it's a great secret to find. And that is why it's so fantastic. That and the rather significant detail of its views. If you like flat, open plains and the ability to see as far as the horizon stretches, go somewhere else. If, though, you prefer giant limestone escarpments that rear up behind the trees, irregularly furrowed hillsides turned purple in spring by a sea of bluebells and like the idea of what might lie over the top of any one of those hills, Woodend Farm will be the place to ponder the thought.

The campsite just squeezes into the south-western fringe of the Yorkshire Dales National Park, where the white rose of the county meets the red rose of Lancashire. The landscape around is outstanding and there is something about the hills, the limestone outcrops bursting from their green coats, that makes you want to explore the next dale, next moor and next lane, whichever county it might be in.

Woodend Farm Campsite is cosy. It has to be, because the prominent Studrigg Scar and Long Scar (which make the eyes open so wide, even the weariest traveller wouldn't need matchsticks) do indeed scar the landscape, their bulk making the campsite feel small and intimate. That's not to say that the site is crowded; each camper has plenty of space, but with hills that look suspiciously like mountains, you can't help but feel pleased to be tucked between the trees in the valley with the tiny Austwick Beck bubbling past your door rather than pitched up on top of the Scar.

Above: Caravanning at Woodend Farm

Individual hardstanding pitches are raised above the brook, making it a great site to enjoy the views even in the depths of winter when the frost plays games with the sunlight over the hills. A large grass field caters for summer visitors who don't require hook-ups and provides enough space for children to play football without fear of reprisals from concerned 'van owners. In spring, lambs cavort around the fields in the valley and up on the bank behind the campsite, where the stone walls keep them from straying to greener grass (most of the time).

Left: Views of the countryside from Woodend Farm

Margaret and Edward Hird have been farming the land at Woodend for a lifetime. They've been showing the baby animals to excited children staying on the site for over 35 years, and, while the lambs of the seventies have long since seen the mint sauce, the children are still returning, now with their own offspring, to see the latest flock dance in the fields. It's a comforting cycle, one that shows life moving on and how the beauty of the place and the friendliness of the people gets under the skin and works magic in the hearts of campers.

But it's not just the campsite that impresses old-timers and newcomers alike. The Yorkshire Dales, with their assortment of peaks, coves, the greenest of green pastures and bleakest of fells, and unique geological features do impetuously force visitors to return. While the three peaks of Ingleborough (this one does 'hide' over the top and round the corner from Woodend Farm), Whernside and Pen-y-Ghent look harmless enough on the bluest of summer afternoons, they've caught out many a walker on desperate days. They are certainly imposing, both to the fell-runner up for the ultimate of challenges or to the onlooker whose only thought is never to be found at the top of the plateau-shaped peaks.

If you consider yourself an onlooker, then you could do worse than to take a circular tour from the campsite. Taking in Ribblesdale and the road from Ingleton to the Ribblehead Viaduct is one of the most spectacular drives you could possibly find. However, being conscious of filling the clear Dales air with stagnant exhaust fumes, it's a good flat route for cyclists too. Sometimes, it can feel as if you're the only person in England and you're glad to be alone until you reach the meeting point of two roads with the giant viaduct. Here, the world meets to enjoy the views, paddle in the Ribble or picnic in the most open of self-provided restaurants.

Woodend Farm

Austwick, North Yorkshire, LA2 8DH

01524 251296

www.woodendcampsite.co.uk

enquiries@woodendcampsite.co.uk

Opening times: Open all year

Facilities: Ten hardstanding plus additional grass pitches, hook-ups (though less hook-ups than pitches), hot showers, toilets, dishwashing, chemical toilet disposal point. Dogs welcome.

How to get there: From the A65, turn off for Austwick and take the road through the village signed for Horton. The campsite is 1 mile from Austwick on the right.

Food & drink: The Gamecock Inn (www.gamecockinn.co.uk) in the centre of Austwick serves good food using local produce but with a French theme running through the menu; the owner trained as a chef in France.

Nearby attractions: The caves at Ingleborough are filled with a lunar landscape of strange limestone formations, made from thousands of years of dripping calcite deposits. For outdoor wonders, Malham Cove and Gordale Scar provide dramatic scenes, with one of the best-preserved limestone pavements in the world sitting at the top of the Cove.

Alternative campsite: Orcaber Farm (www.caravancamping yorkshiredales.co.uk, tel.: 07800 624994). Less than a mile from Woodend Campsite, it has almost as good views but sits on the southern side of the A65.

Top: Peaceful Woodend Farm, well away from the noisy main roads
Bottom Left: The Yorkshire Dales – perfect walking country
Bottom Right: The entrance to the farm

Usha Gap
North Yorkshire

It seems as though the road through Swaledale is the longest route in the world when you're travelling along it. It doesn't take up much space on a map – just a few inches – but pull out the meandering curves like a piece of string and actually it's a whole lot longer; almost as long as a piece of string. Add in the fact that you can't drive fast along it and it does indeed go on forever. Actually, you won't want to drive fast because that would mean missing some of the most beautiful scenery that Yorkshire – indeed, England – has to offer. The changing landscape is so spectacular that you have to stop every now and again to take it all in, as if there is too much beauty to appreciate it all in one go.

Above: Arriving at Usha Gap

Swaledale is one of the most northerly of the Yorkshire Dales, virtually at the top of the National Park. It runs from east to west, parallel with the more southerly Wensleydale, and its landscape changes as the river runs east. The Swale eventually runs into the River Ouse close to the city of York, causing all kinds of problems for the city residents when the river's in spate, but here in Swaledale the river trips over stones, gathering pebbles as it dances on its merry way without a care in the world. At the eastern end of the dale, close to Richmond, the hills unfold with a gentle beauty, the green of the high-sided pastures vivid and vibrant. As you head back, ever so slowly, towards the river's source, the green remains intense on the lower slopes while the rougher moorland hues rise higher and higher until you feel the hills soaring above. The ribbon road is punctuated by little hamlets oozing a communal spirit; each village is the one you'd like to move to until the next appears, which seems better than the last, and so it goes on.

It's at the western end, where the landscape receives the best of both green dale and high moor, that the campsite at Usha Gap resides. Pronounced 'Oeusha' in the same way you'd ask for eggs in France (*oeufs*), it is run by a friendly couple, Philip and Louise Metcalfe, Philip having grown up on the farm. They are people of the field; Philip's parents, who worked the farm and campsite before Philip and his wife took over, live next door. Hence, it's fair to say the family has seen many a snowdrift melt and new spring dawn, most of them from the same window, having lived in the house since both father and son were the tiniest of

Right: The village of Muker, Swaledale

tots. In that time, the family has seen a lot of campers come and go, and return too. It's little wonder; it would be hard to find a more lovely place in the Dales to set up home for a while.

The campsite is small. It's a strip of grass right beside a shallow beck, which flows into the Swale a little farther downstream and is the perfect depth for rolling up the trouser legs and refreshing the toes, in summer at least. If I said the road runs past, many might be put off. True enough, it does, but we're not talking either the speed or width of the M1. This is the same road that takes a long time to drive along, where traffic is scant and tends to be ambling. The house and basic (but clean) facilities are on the other side of the road, together with an additional field that's used when the campsite gets really busy around bank holidays. Families with small children worried about road crossing could use this field but, frankly, the site by the stream is far prettier and more fun for playing.

If there are extra bonus points for the campsite, aside from the incredible views of the hills on either side, the location just half a mile out of lovely Muker village, the proximity to the Pennine Way and the sheep that frequent the hillside, it's because it stays open all year. When other campsites have mothballed the reception, Usha Gap lets you continue camping, taking full advantage of the beautiful autumn and winter scenes, quieter roads and quieter everything. It's the perfect time to stretch the legs and see the legacy of past Swaledale residents – a mass of stone walls that climb the hillsides and more tiny stone cattle barns than you can count. They make Swaledale what it is and why we all come to visit.

Usha Gap Caravans and Camping

Muker, Swaledale, North Yorkshire, DL11 6DW

01748 886110

www.ushagap.co.uk

info@ushagap.co.uk

Opening times: Open all year

Facilities: 24 pitches (no hook-ups), showers, toilets, washbasins, electric shaver points, chemical toilet disposal point, drying room, laundry room, dishwashing.

How to get there: From M6, take junction 38, then A685, signed Brough. Turn at B6270 for Muker and Reeth, site is a quarter of a mile past Thwaite on right. From M1/A1, take Scotch Corner junction of A1, A6108 through Richmond, turn right onto B6270, signed for Reeth, continue along Swaledale, site is half a mile past Muker on left. The B6270 is perfectly wide but slow and winding; anticipate it taking some time, sit back and enjoy the views, remembering that the locals are not all on holiday and do need to get about.

Food & drink: The Farmers Arms (tel.: 01748 886297). Nice traditional pub in the centre of Muker serving real ales and good home-cooked food. Dogs and muddy boots welcome.

Nearby attractions: Explore the beautiful villages of Swaledale: Muker, Healaugh and Reeth are particularly pretty. Head over the Buttertubs Pass for incredible views of Swaledale (road is fine for motorhomes) and some spectacular scenery. The village of Hawes has lots to do, including a visit to the famous Wensleydale Creamery to watch the cheese being made and to sample lots!

Alternative campsite: Scabba Wath Campsite (tel.: 01748 884601). Small, basic campsite farther along the dale, 2 miles west of Reeth.

Top Left: The shallow waters of the beck that borders the campsite
Bottom Left: Swaledale is ideal for touring and exploring
Right: Typical Swaledale scenes – a Swaledale sheep and characteristic barn

Finchale Abbey
County Durham

People have been holidaying at Finchale for hundreds of years. Not at the caravan site, admittedly, but the 13th-century Benedictine abbey, as a dependent of Durham Cathedral, was used by monks from the city to rest awhile from their habitual religious tasks. They enjoyed a little more freedom during their stay than they were usually allowed, treating it as a modern-day retreat. With the abbey now in ruins, a result of the 16th-century dissolution of the monasteries, it's the caravan site that's now the retreat, an adults-only park free from children tearing around on scooters and pestering parents for ice cream.

St Godric first resided at the site early in the 12th century, before it became an abbey. Living as a hermit, he allegedly slept for most of his life outdoors, rejecting finer comforts, and did more travelling around Europe than many caravanners do today. Nevertheless, tents are not allowed at Finchale Abbey and caravan beds are far more comfortable now; but if you really want to fill a bag with straw and rest your head outdoors, that's up to you.

Returning from his European pilgrimages and deciding to set up base, St Godric certainly knew how to pick a great location. Finchale (pronounced 'Finkle') Abbey was built on a bend in the River Wear, a waterway that curls its way back and forth through Durham and out to the North Sea. Steep cliffs on the other side of the river at Finchale somehow or other manage to give life

to a woodland, the tree roots clinging to what little earth there is. All in all, with the abbey and the caravan site being on the end of the no-through road, it's a very peaceful place.

Above: Pitches right next to the ruins at Finchale Abbey Caravan Park

Behind the touring site a residents-only eco holiday village has been created. If that sounds horrendous, don't worry; it's merely a collection of timber chalets that is kept entirely separate from the touring area and doesn't interfere with it. Grass and hardstanding pitches for tourers are sited in the same bend in the river as the abbey. While there's an element of columns and rows in the pitch layout, it's not particularly noticeable, with some 'vans positioned by the walls of the abbey and others parked at differing angles. A gentle hill rises up to the side of the pitches, which has been left open and wild for visitors – and the resident guinea fowl – to wander about on.

Left: The ruins of Finchale Abbey

Though the abbey, managed by English Heritage, is directly in front of the site and clearly visible from all the pitches – dominating the foreground, in fact – it is fenced off from the park, as it's open to the general public. The ruins are mysteriously beautiful; the stone walls still retaining magnificent gothic arches and empty windows where the sunlight plays tricks with long, shaped shadows. Its very being creates an aura that's calm and reflective and, coupled with the peaceful river's tune, Sunday mornings are easy.

The river is accessible directly in front of the campsite, where a small grassy area is laid out with picnic tables. Canoeing, swimming (though it's shallow in places) and fishing are allowed on the river, with a 2-mile stretch of riverbank for anglers (day tickets are available from the small on-site shop) suitable for both fly and coarse fishing with plump brown trout waiting for a fly.

Those who prefer not to dabble in the river can walk alongside it, by crossing the footbridge and taking a wander in the riverside country park. This is a fine way to see the upper reaches of the river and the densely wooded valley that it winds through. The Weardale Way also runs straight past the site and will take you into the centre of Durham, allowing you to leave your car behind.

To get back to nature without too much strenuous exercise, take the Weardale Railway that runs steam trains between Stanhope and Wolsingham, one of the least-known dales in the north of England yet with beautiful scenery; this could have saved St Godric a lot of walking too.

Finchale Abbey Caravan Park

Finchale Abbey Farm, County Durham, DH1 5SH

0191 386 6528

www.finchaleabbey.co.uk

godricawatson@hotmail.com

Opening times: Open all year

Facilities: 50 pitches with hook-ups, modern showers/toilet facilities, shaver points and hairdryers, dishwashing, chemical toilet disposal point, shop, small cafe. Dogs welcome.

How to get there: Junction 63 of A1(M), A167 signed Durham. At 'Pity Me' roundabout, turn left to Red House, right to Newton Grange and left to Brasside. At Brasside, turn left onto the road leading to Finchale Abbey.

Food & drink: Nothing spectacular locally. Head to Durham for a good selection of restaurants and pubs. The Durham City Farmers' Market takes place on the third Thursday of each month in the Market Place.

Nearby attractions: Crook Hall Gardens in Durham provide a peaceful retreat in the centre of the city. Beamish Open Air Museum, 7 miles from Finchale Abbey, takes you back a couple of hundred years to experience life in a bygone era. Those in need of some retail therapy can spend away at the Metro Centre in Gateshead, 15 miles from the campsite.

Alternative campsite: Durham Grange Caravan Club Site (www.caravanclub.co.uk, tel.: 0191 384 4778). Open to non-members, a standard club site but with some noise from the A1.

Left: Sunlight plays tricks through empty windows of the abbey
Top Right: The caravan park is beside the River Wear
Bottom Right: There are views of the ruins from the caravan site

Highside Farm
County Durham

Highside Farm, you could say, is almost exclusive – deliberately and unashamedly so. In one of those rare occasions when commercialism plays second fiddle to quality, the campsite actually insists upon allowing fewer units on site than it's licensed for. That's perhaps no bad thing, because, as a small site, a few extra units could make everyone feel a little cramped. However, owners Richard and Stephanie have seen the good sense to allow those who do stay a little bit of extra room.

It's exclusive, too, because it's people that count, not 'vans, hence they are counted – a maximum of eight guests on site at any one time. That might irritate the odd couple passing by who haven't booked and like the look of the place (and they *would* like the look of the place) and the countryside that surrounds it. But there's a simple answer to that – book in advance. Of course, Richard and Stephanie will gladly put you up if you happen to be passing and there is space available, but the chances are you will need to book because the location is truly spectacular.

Highside Farm, as its name indicates, is on the side of a high hill in the North Pennines. It's in an Area of Outstanding Natural Beauty, a designated term that makes the landscape equally significant as a National Park, yet it's not been granted that status, so fewer tourists flock to the hilltops in quite the same way as they do to nearby neighbours, such as the Lake District or the Yorkshire Dales. If there is an air of one-upmanship though, the North Pennines was the first area in Britain to be designated a UNESCO European Geopark. It's a long-winded title, but in essence it's a place where the geology of the region plays an important role in supporting sustainable development for the future. Put simply, it's special.

Above: Richard and Stephanie's sheep at the farm

And it is the geology that we should thank for the views from the campsite, where hills bulge and valleys fold more frequently than a tidal wave. The farm is one of half a dozen houses that sit on a ledge, the grassy slopes continuing to rise behind them. All around are views of other hills and valleys – Lunedale and Teesdale in particular – some green, some brown where the moorlands rise up. The obligatory sheep dot the landscape, and at Highside Farm these are special too.

With just 16 acres, it's more of a smallholding than a farm, where Richard and Stephanie rear rare-breed animals, such as the local Teeswater sheep, a breed almost extinct prior to the Second World War. It was a conscious decision when they arrived nearly 20 years ago to utilize the meadows rich in wild flowers and to provide the best care to the animals (rare-breed pigs and Shorthorn cattle followed). Says Richard, 'The farming methods that we have used over the years have enabled us to restore the botanical diversity of the farm, with our hay meadows having as many as fifty species in flower at once. Teesdale is becoming quite a centre for botanical tourism and has species of flower unique within England, such as the Blue Gentian.'

A natural ethos runs through the farm to the campsite. Richard and Stephanie like campers who care for their environment, asking 'van owners to use septic-tank-friendly chemicals and limit the use of electricity; a kettle, TV, Xbox (seriously, you won't need one while you're here) and hair curlers all on at the same time will blow the trip. In all, it's a site for guests who want to get out and about walking, cycling or fishing to make the most of the location, to sit and enjoy the scenery and paint, read or just chill. Whatever you do, you must look at the view.

Should, heaven forbid, you tire of it, then take a wander through Lunedale and the nearby Grassholme Reservoir. The Pennine Way cuts across its western end and takes you to other notable hay meadows brimming with wildflowers including those once owned by Hannah Hauxwell, who came to prominence in the 1980s with a series of television programmes about her life in the Dales. It's now a nature reserve where visitors can learn more about the importance of this upland landscape. Alternatively, nip into Middleton-in-Teesdale and follow the road to Alston in neighbouring Cumbria: it has to be one of the best roads in the country for continual good views.

Highside Farm

Bowbank, Middleton-in-Teesdale,
County Durham, DL12 0NT

01833 640135

www.highsidefarm.co.uk

Opening times: Easter to end of September

Facilities: Four pitches (maximum of eight people on site in total) for 'vans no more than 6 metres (20 feet) in length, two hook-ups, shower, toilets, dishwashing.

How to get there: From M6 junction 38, A685 to Brough, B6276, signed Middleton-in-Teesdale, site is approximately 12 miles from Brough on right. From A1 Scotch Corner junction, A66 to Barnard Castle, B6277 Barnard Castle to Middleton-in-Teesdale road, turn onto B6276, signed Brough. Site is 1 mile on left (caravans should drive 25 yards farther up the hill and turn in the layby to approach from the right, as it's a tight turn).

Food & drink: The Fox and Hounds (tel.: 01833 650241) at Cotherstone serves meals using locally sourced produce. Middleton-in-Teesdale Fish and Chip Shop, 1 mile from the campsite, offers excellent food, including homemade pies.

Nearby attractions: The Pennine Way runs close to Highside Farm. Middleton-in-Teesdale is lovely. High Force Waterfall, on the River Tees, is spectacular. Hannah's Meadow Nature Reserve near Blackton Reservoir is 5 miles from the campsite (a farm once owned by Hannah Hauxwell, who farmed using entirely traditional practices).

Alternative campsite: Doe Park Caravan Site (tel.: 01833 650302). A clean and friendly grass site on the outskirts of Cotherstone, but without the views.

Top Left: Spring daffodils welcome visitors to Highside Farm
Top Right: A caravan parked at the site
Bottom: Views around Highside Farm

Kielder Village
Northumberland

Few man-made attractions match up to nature's ability to create the finest features. Kielder Water and the Border Forest Park are different, however. Nature has grabbed the opportunity and made this entirely manufactured landscape one of her own; you would never be aware just by gazing at the skyline that 40 years ago this area was carved up by diggers, dumper trucks and hordes of construction workers walking on the lake floor. That is, with the exception of one thing – the large wall of the dam, which you only really notice as you leave, holding back the 200 million cubic metres of water that calmly sit in their rightful place.

The construction of Kielder Water began in 1975 as a necessary measure to keep the wheels turning on the north-east's booming industry. It took six years to complete and another two years to fill, but things changed and the anticipated capacity wasn't needed. Some capacity it is, too – the largest man-made lake in the UK, holding the largest amount of water of any of the country's reservoirs. While the water is still there in case of emergencies, it's become a giant playground for lovers of the great outdoors. It's shape, with inlets from forest streams and spurs, coupled with the wild landscape and the trees that have grown up around, now makes it look as if it's been there for eternity.

It's not just the lake that's had the human touch. Kielder Forest is all man-made, too; a swathe of pine trees that covers nearly 240 square miles of Northumberland hills.

Kielder Water spreads itself in the centre of this forest and the moorlands peeking up above the canopy shows just how much space per person everybody gets here. The Campaign to Protect Rural England has officially marked Kielder Water and Forest Park as England's most tranquil spot – the perfect place to put a campsite.

Above: Kielder Caravan and Camping Site

Kielder Caravan and Camping Site is at the far north-western tip of the lake, 3 miles shy of the Scottish border and a fraction out of Kielder village. It's a forest site rather than lakeside, taking advantage of a grassy break in the trees, which makes the site altogether nicely enclosed while still retaining distant views of the moorlands to avoid feeling claustrophobic.

It's essentially a game of two halves: the hardstanding touring pitches are the first that you come to; due to the amount of rainfall that the site receives, there are

Left: Kielder Water and Forest

no grass pitches for motorhomes and caravans. The other half of the site, over the small river bridge and past the facility buildings, is reserved for tents. The shower and toilet facilities were totally refurbished in November 2015, but caravanners might prefer to use their own, topping up from the fresh water supply that comes straight from the hill.

Kielder Campsite is a community project. It's owned and run by the people of Kielder in order to keep England's most remote village thriving. The village is a good base from which to begin exploring the area, with Kielder Castle the focal point and one-time seat of the Duke of Northumberland. The 26-mile Lakeside Way takes walkers around the perimeter of the lake, but for those who want to get onto the water you can bring your own boat, canoe or kayak (the vessel must be insured) and there are many professional clubs in the area that provide water-based activities. Situated on the south-western flank of the lake, the park offers sailing, waterskiing, windsurfing and the opportunity for anglers to hire motorboats to fish from the water rather than from the bank (although that's available too).

Cyclists have all kinds of trails to explore around the lake and through the forest, with a mountain-bike skills area by Kielder Castle. The natural world is abundant here, with over half the population of England's red squirrels foraging in the woods and the chance to see ospreys plummeting to the water in the hope of catching lunch. Close to the village, the Kielder Salmon Centre has a breeding programme; you can book tours to find out about the conservation work.

For all the daytime activities, night-time is still the best: with the lowest level of light pollution in the country, this is the place to watch the sun set and the stars twinkle – and you can do so easily with the naked eye or with a little extra help at the Kielder Observatory.

Kielder Village Caravan and Campsite

Kielder Village, Hexham, Northumberland, NE48 1BX

01434 250291

www.kieldercampsite.co.uk

kieldercampsite@btinternet.com

Opening times: Mid-March to October

Facilities: 22 hardstanding pitches for caravans & motorhomes (additional pitches for tents), hook-ups, showers, toilets, washbasins, dishwashing, chemical toilet disposal point, small shop with basic essentials. (Take insect repellent in the summer for the midges.) 4 non-serviced camping pods to hire.

How to get there: A69 to Hexham, A6079 to Wall. One mile past Wall, turn onto B6320 to Bellingham. Follow the signs for Kielder Water (left turn just before the town centre). Site is on the right at the far end of the lake, through Kielder village, approximately 10 miles from the Tower Knowe Visitor Centre. Petrol stations are scarce; fill up before you enter Kielder Forest and Water Park.

Food & drink: The Cafe in the Castle at Kielder Castle for morning coffee, lunchtime snacks and afternoon tea. The Angler's Arms (tel.: 01434 250072) in Kielder village isn't the prettiest of pubs, but they serve plenty of simple, hearty food to fill a gap.

Nearby attractions: Make the most of Kielder's remote location and take advantage of the space. Take a trip on board The Osprey (from Leaplish Water Park or Tower Knowe) for a tour of the lake from the water.

Alternative campsite: Leaplish Waterside Park (www.leaplish.co.uk, tel.: 01434 251000). On the edge of the lake with all watersports facilities and land-based activities (high ropes, climbing, cycle hire) to hand. Pitches are under the trees and some with lake views. It can get very busy and quite noisy.

Top Left: Sheltered pitches at Kielder
Top Right: Caravans at Kielder
Bottom: The vastness of Kielder Water

Haltwhistle
Northumberland

When the Romans were in town, they certainly knew how to live. They knew how to build, too, and how to fight. When Hadrian built his wall in AD122 to keep out the harassing Picts who were getting up his nose and to show his military muscle to anyone who liked the idea of invading, more than 10,000 Roman soldiers stood guard. Fighting off a few invasions, the soldiers lived in the garrisons along Hadrian's Wall for over 200 years before packing up their bags and leaving Britain for good.

Above: Wild flowers adorning the 'dog walk'

The Romans' legacy is legendary, the remains of the 73-mile wall now serve as a reminder of the days when life and labour were cheap. Could you imagine anyone taking on such a project now? In today's quieter times, it also serves as a marching ground for wandering walkers pitting themselves against the invasion of a north wind and as an outdoor photographic studio for tourists eager to have their picture taken pointing at a pile of stones to prove that they were there.

To follow in the footsteps of Hadrian's men, the Hadrian's Wall Path runs alongside the wall. The seasonal (March to September) AD122 Hadrian's Wall Country Bus also runs much of the length of the trail, stopping at many of the important Roman sites and linking up with other local bus routes, so walkers can take a break.

The Camping and Caravanning Club site, 2½ miles south of Haltwhistle, is slap bang in the centre of the trail for those on the march. Four miles from the wall, it stands next to another great institution, the River Tyne; actually the River South Tyne to be exact, before it meets the North Tyne (from Kielder Water, **see** page 57) at Hexham to form one giant ribbon. Past the campsite, the South Tyne flows through the beautiful North Pennines countryside, where the fells meet the luscious lower slopes of the valley, rich with wildlife and farm animals. It's a very quiet rural area with a handful of tiny villages, where noises are created by the birds, the river and your footsteps alone.

With this landscape as a background, campers pitch in a clearing of Bellister Wood, part of the Bellister Castle Estate owned by the National Trust. The trees take the glare out of the sun without overshadowing the entire site, and 'vans can park either in the more open central grass area or around the edges with a little more shade.

Right: The River South Tyne, which runs past the campsite

There are some hardstanding pitches where 'vans tend to line up; without any grass in this area of the campsite it can feel a little like a car park, but it does have the best views of the river. Shaped in a long thin strip, it's the area farthest from the entrance that has the quietest and grassiest pitches. They back onto a spinney where the scent of wild garlic in summer is enough to reach for the barbecue and start cooking. The wild garlic's white flowers smother the ground, thriving on the banks in the mottled shade.

At the far end of the site is the 'dog walk'. If you don't have a dog, pretend you have one or ignore the terminology and go for a wander anyway. It's one of the most beautiful 'dog walks' on a campsite, with paths leading this way and that through the trees that go on forever and wild flowers that fill the ground with colour. There's also access to the river every few yards, providing places to play on the giant pebbles smoothed by the passage of time and to paddle. The river is suitable for fly-fishing, offered to anyone staying on site with a rod licence.

The lanes around the site are quiet for walking too, and for anyone who doesn't want to join the trail of walkers on Hadrian's Wall, there are many other footpaths across the fields close by, including the Pennine Way.

For a Roman education, head to Vindolanda, 6 miles from the campsite; this former Roman fort is home to the largest collection of buildings belonging to the empire makers. Archaeologists are still digging and scraping back the soil to uncover further treasures of the past and visitors can chat to them as they work. Volunteers are sometimes needed to help with the painstaking, knee-bending toil. Housesteads Fort, on the other side of the wall, is one of the best-preserved forts, illustrating what it was like to be a Roman soldier and how they lived.

Haltwhistle Camping and Caravanning Club Site

Burnfoot Park Village, Haltwhistle, Northumberland, NE49 0JP

01434 320106

www.campingandcaravanningclub.co.uk

Opening times: March to end of October

Facilities: 50 pitches with hook-ups, immaculate amenity building with showers, toilets and washbasins, shaver points, chemical waste disposal point, motorhome service point, laundry facilities, dishwashing, gas exchange, dog walk, small shop. Dogs welcome.

How to get there: Turn off A69 on Haltwhistle bypass, signed Alston & Coanwood. One and a half miles from main road, turn first right (before the village of Park). Site entrance is at the bottom of the short hill on right.

Food & drink: Greenhead Tea Rooms (tel.: 01697 747400), in the village of Greenhead, is a 10-minute drive from the campsite and a 5-minute walk from Hadrian's Wall and the Pennine Way. It has a great reputation for using locally-sourced produce to make delicious food. The tearoom is on the South West Northumberland Tasty Trail if you want to tour a route of great foodie places.

Nearby attractions: Take a trip across the county border to Alston in Cumbria, which is not only the highest market town in England but also has a cobbled main street. For further Roman exploration visit the Roman Army Museum at Greenhead to learn about Hadrian and his soldiers.

Alternative campsite: Hadrian's Wall Campsite (www.hadrianswallcampsite.co.uk, tel.: 01434 320495). An open terraced site on the hills and across the road from Hadrian's Wall, 2 miles from Haltwhistle.

Left: Bluebells in Bellister Wood
Top Right: The campsite, set in a clearing in Bellister Wood
Bottom Right: Lots of opportunities to enjoy the Northumberland countryside

Church Farm Organics
Merseyside

Searching for campsites in Merseyside is like looking for the proverbial needle, perhaps not surprising given its industrial heritage. So to find one with the attributes for a cool caravanner is more than gratifying, as they get to visit an area otherwise lost from the camping agenda.

Above: Geese at Church Farm

The Wirral peninsula is more associated with shipbuilding and soap-making than unhitching a caravan. Green, open spaces, wild habitats, golden sands and attractive sea views don't come high on the list of known features when you ask a non-resident about the borough. However, Church Farm sits on the pretty west coast, surrounded by the Wirral Country Park of grassland and coastal heathland.

The owner of Church Farm, Steve Ledsham, was once working on the other side of the Mersey, putting out fires for the City of Liverpool. After injuring his back he was told he'd never be a fireman again, so when the farm came up for auction in the early 1990s, Steve leaped at the chance to buy it. His heart was in horticulture, always growing his own vegetables without chemicals, so it was a natural progression to convert the farm to organic status, long before eating organic food became trendy. The farm has been organic ever since, selling their home-grown fruit and vegetables in the farm shop along with other locally sourced produce. Steve's aim is to have all the fruit, vegetables and meat supplied from within a 25-mile radius, an aspect that's helped him to win the 'Best Farm Shop' award in the past.

The 60-acre farm is a hit with children because of the many activities – feeding sheep, collecting eggs and finding out about the other animals. Those who stay on the campsite are allowed to wander around the farm and visit the animals free of charge, while day visitors are obliged to pay. There are regular children's activities organized throughout the year too, such as Easter egg hunts or trips to the organic Christmas tree forest. For grown-ups simply appreciating the views over the River Dee and the Welsh hills should be enough, but the farm also runs a cafe with cosy sofas and log-burning stoves where you can chill out and warm up while tucking into a frothy coffee and the newspapers.

The campsite is a small five-van certificated site (for which you must be a member of the Camping and

Right: The farm shop at Church Farm

Caravanning Club) that's tucked into a corner against a hedge. There are no views of the estuary from here and it's quite close to the main road, so you have to expect a certain amount of noise. It does mean the site is sheltered from the wind, however, and once you're in the farm park, there are superb views out to sea.

When location is key, this site hits the mark. Travelling from the M56, you drive first through a series of small towns, some of which might make you wonder why you've chosen to visit. Then the houses stop and the open space really begins – Thurstaston Common, an area of parkland, wood and heath with Thurstaston Hill at its peak. It's designated an SSSI (Site of Special Scientific Interest), as is the River Dee and much of the Wirral Country Park that follows the Wirral Way, a 12-mile path for walkers and cyclists. The country park drops down to the sandy beaches at the mouth of the Dee. Those with a brisk step can head out to the Hilbre Islands, a couple of miles offshore; they're reachable at low tide from West Kirby and you need to make a swift exit before you get caught short and need to swap boots for flippers, but the three red-rocked islands are a bird sanctuary and attract colonies of Atlantic grey seals, as well as being noted for their plant life.

The Ness Botanic Gardens and RSPB Reserve are both on the west side of the Wirral too, but venturing to the other side of the M53 will take you to Port Sunlight, the village created by Lord Lever for the workers at his soap factory. The Lady Lever Art Gallery, with its reputable collection of permanent and temporary exhibitions, is also at Port Sunlight.

Hoylake on the north-west coast is a picture-postcard town, and from there or West Kirby (closer to the campsite and within cycling distance) you can catch the train to the big city for a taste of Liverpool's waterfront.

Church Farm Organics

Church Lane, Thurstaston, Wirral, CH61 0HW

0151 648 7838

www.churchfarm.org.uk

sales@churchfarm.org.uk

Opening times: Campsite open all year; farm shop and cafe varying times according to the season

Facilities: 5 pitches in a Certificated Site, hook-ups, toilets, showers, disabled facilities, chemical toilet disposal point, farm shop, cafe.

How to get there: Junction 16 on M56, A540 through Heswall, signed Hoylake. At Thurstaston, turn left signed for Wirral Country Park (ignore all previous signs for the park). Follow the one-way road round to the left, past the church. Church Farm is 100 metres from the church on the right.

Food & drink: The farm shop and cafe on site during the day. For evening meals, the Cottage Loaf, 50 metres from the site, serves filling but ordinary fare, while the Jug and Bottle at Heswall is regarded as more of a gastro-pub.

Nearby attractions: A visit to Liverpool is not complete without taking a ferry across the Mersey. Catch one from the Woodside (Birkenhead) or Seacombe (Wallasey) ferry terminals on The Wirral.

Alternative campsites: Wirral Country Park Caravan Club Site (www.caravanclub.co.uk, tel.: 0151 648 5228). One mile from Church Farm and open to non-members, the site has similar views of the River Dee and the Welsh hills. It's quieter than Church Farm but not quite so hip.

Top Left: A sandpit for the children at Church Farm
Bottom Left: Thurstaston Church
Right: Views of the River Dee and North Wales from Church Farm

Midlands

Rowter Farm
Derbyshire

It's impossible to understand how parts of the Peak District haven't imploded, such is the extent of honeycomb caves beneath the surface. For however many people there are walking the ridges above, there will almost certainly be someone delving into the cavernous spaces below, their head torch lighting up several million years of history. The High Peak is an area where for potholes read subterraneous caverns, rather than the usual suspension-busting pits in tarmac.

And some of the best – and deepest – of these caves are between Castleton and the oddly named village of Sparrowpit. Up above all of this underground activity, oblivious to the world beneath them, a large herd of cattle and several hundred sheep graze contentedly on the sweet grass that caps the hills. In among all this, campers fill their kettles and prepare for a fresh brew while admiring the long-distance panorama and the daredevil attributes of the paragliders riding on the hot air rising off Rushup Edge – a ridge so steep that people do anything but rush up it.

The High Peak is certainly one of the most popular playgrounds for outdoor enthusiasts or obsessives. And Rowter Farm Campsite is in the middle of it all. A working farm where the sheep and cattle play their part in the landscape in equilibrium with the fields that they graze, it sits at the top of Winnats Pass, a canyon that makes onlookers draw breath as much as it makes cars wince. Dropping like a stone below, you can't actually see the canyon from the campsite – that's reserved for those making their way into Castleton – but you can see just about everything else in the Peak District, at least it feels that way.

Above: Harebells at Winnats Pass

Within the grounds of the farm, the actual campsite area is set a field away from the Sparrowpit to Castleton road, up a long track. It's no more than a grassy field (which requires levelling devices) enclosed by some fine Derbyshire stone walls and hedges to protect campers from the potential hilltop winds. There are some very basic facilities in the farmyard and that's about it, really – except for the views, and they make up for five-star hairdryers anyday. Every which way you turn, there's something different to look at. It would take a long stay if you chose a different outlook every day, whether it's the long views over Longcliff, the sheep-filled fields and stone walls one way, Rushup Edge another, the rugged slopes of Mam Tor or the far-stretching panorama around Lose Hill.

With so much breathtaking beauty, it's no wonder people want to get out and about. Mountain bikers have any number of opportunities to push the pedal either up steep slopes or along more gentle trails around the High Peak reservoirs. There isn't a day goes by without seeing a climber dipping their fingers in a pocket of chalk and edging their way up some craggy cliff face, whether it's at nearby Winnats Pass or ever so slightly farther afield on the harder gritstone surfaces at Stoney Middleton and Stanedge. Potholers can select their route according to ability and make for caves with obscure names, such as Giant's Hole (given the local's affectionate term for Peak Cavern is The Devil's Arse, the mind boggles).

If all this activity or even a walk along the Limestone Way that runs close to the campsite sounds far too strenuous, then you can visit one of the four caverns open to the public that are all within a mile of Rowter Farm. Peak Cavern is a completely natural hole in the ground and the only one in the village of Castleton; Speedwell Cavern, at the foot of Winnats Pass includes an underground canal where visitors can take a boat trip through the cave; while both Treak Cliff and Blue John Mine are the ones to visit to see incredible stalactites and stalagmites pulling on the roof and lifting the floor.

While the Limestone Way moseys south, Edale is the place to join the Pennine Way for a northerly walk. Edale is a mere hop, skip and jump across Mam Tor from Rowter Farm and, standing on top of the ridge, you can see right along the Edale valley.

With all this activity, you're sure to get a good night's sleep. But if the wind should keep you awake at night, well, you can always count sheep.

Rowter Farm

Castleton, Derbyshire, S33 8WA

01433 620271

Opening times: Easter to October

Facilities: Very basic toilets and showers, dishwashing area, rubbish collection. No hook-ups. Dogs welcome.

How to get there: From A623 Chapel-en-le-Frith to Baslow road, turn onto road signed for Castleton and the Caverns. After approximately 4 miles, the farm track to Rowter Farm Campsite is on your right. It's poorly signed; take care approaching as the gate is always shut and you need to pull off the road while opening it. Caravans should not approach through Castleton and Winnats Pass.

Food & drink: Castleton is a mile from the site and has a vast selection of good places to eat and drink, from quaint tea rooms to pubs and hotels.

Nearby attractions: Take a tour around the High Peak villages, including Tideswell where it's enormous 14th-century parish church is known as the 'Cathedral of the Peak' and dominates the centre of the village. Hop on the train at Hope station and make the short but stunning journey to Edale. The ruins of Peveril Castle (English Heritage) are 'next door' to Rowter Farm.

Alternative campsite: Coopers Campsite (tel.: 01433 670372) in Edale is even beyond basic in terms of facilities but still has some good views.

Top Left: Basic camping at Rowter Farm
Bottom Left: Inquisitive sheep at Rowter Farm
Right: Paragliders making for Rushup Edge

Bakewell
Derbyshire

As Britain's busiest national park, it's pretty tricky to find a spot you can call your own for a few hours in the Peak District; somewhere away from the world busily rushing to make the most of a weekend getaway from the massive urban conurbations that hem in the uplands. As city life expands around the peripheries, it feels as though the hills are being squeezed closer together, pushed ever higher, ready to explode like some volcanic eruption, spitting and spewing out the people that have encroached on its once bleak moors and escarpments. Not that there's any danger of volcanic activity these days, the last eruption in the Peak District took place several million years ago – long before it became Britain's first national park, a mere 65 years ago.

In fact, geologically speaking, the Peak District has had a lot to contend with over the years – hot lava flows, tropical seas, its fair share of crashing and banging, squeezing, folding, cracking and splitting causing erosion and exposure of its softer underbelly, not to mention several ice ages, the area frozen to its core. As if it hadn't had enough, for the last 400 years, it has had an explosion of tourists coming to marvel at the beautiful results of all the tumultuous activity.

But where is there to go when every bit of land over and under seems to have a walker, cyclist, climber, paraglider, fell-runner or potholer already there? Even the campsites are some of the most popular

in the country and get extraordinarily busy. A field in the middle of nowhere in particular seems to be the best bet.

Above: View of the distant Youlgreave Village from the site

Despite its name, the Camping and Caravanning Club's Bakewell site, open to non-members, is 5 miles from the town and a mile away from the nearest village, Youlgreave. Its isolated position – along a private road – means that the only traffic you see is the comings and goings of your fellow campers and those of the neighbouring small farm campsite. And because it has no toilets or showers, it puts off a lot of fair-weather settlers, but it needn't bother the likes of us 'van owners with our own on-board luxuries.

Set over three fields broken up by hedges, traditional Derbyshire stone walls and small plantations of pine trees, each part of the site feels different. To the rear of the site, half a dozen seasonal pitches shelter below Graftondale that softly rears up behind. In the centre of the site, well-spaced and large hardstanding level pitches cater for the biggest 'vans without the worry of sinking in or the need for digging out. Either side lie sloping all-grass fields, with spectacular views of the pretty village of Youlgreave to the west and a panoramic middle-of-nowhere vista to the east, where only the odd farmstead illustrates human activity. There's no need for uniform rows here, and many of the best sites are, naturally, the ones without hook-ups on the fringes of the grass fields. The campsite managers at Bakewell know the terrain well, so they'll suggest the best way to angle your 'van to maximize the views according to your spot and to capitalize on the sunshine according to your preferences as early bird or late-night diva.

As you would expect, there is plenty of walking on offer. For a short walk make for Youlgreave village to partake in refreshments at a choice of inns, or follow the River Bradford (the one you cross over to reach the campsite) and the Limestone Way. There are footpaths from the campsite that lead to the surrounding hills, too. When brighter lights beckon, the medieval Haddon Hall is the closer of the 'Big Two' estates, the impressive but magnetizing Chatsworth being 5 miles or so farther on. However, don't expect to be alone here, not at weekends, anyway, when the estate paths resemble school-dinner queues. It's little wonder that the town of Bakewell pulls in the tourists, too, with its riverside setting, quaint shops and historic buildings. Thank heavens, then, for the campsite to escape to.

Bakewell Camping and Caravanning Club Site

Hopping Lane, Youlgreave, Bakewell, Derbyshire, DE45 1NA

01629 636555

www.campingandcaravanningclub.co.uk

Opening times: March to end of October

Facilities: 100 pitches, hook-ups, hardstanding and grass pitches, chemical toilet disposal point, water taps, small playground, gas exchange, basic shop, dog walk. Dogs welcome.

How to get there: From A6 Bakewell to Matlock, turn onto B5056 between Rowsley and Haddon Hall. In half a mile bear right, signed Youlgreave. In Youlgreave, turn left by the church into Bradford Road (narrow from here) and over the river bridge. In half a mile turn right up farm track signed for Hopping Farm. Site is quarter of a mile farther on the left.

Food & drink: Chatsworth Estate Farm Shop at Pilsley is one of the best farm shops in the country, with awards to prove it. Stocking a fantastic range of basic provisions and tasty treats, it has local and regional specialities – 60 per cent of the produce comes from the estate itself. You won't need a supermarket at all.

Nearby attractions: Chatsworth Park (www.chatsworth.org) will provide entertainment all day with free access to the estate for walking. There's also the house, gardens and a children's farm. Haddon Hall (www.haddonhall.co.uk) is a more intimate manor house with Elizabethan gardens. The old railway track between Bakewell and Buxton is now the Monsal Trail used by cyclists.

Alternative campsite: Hopping Farm Caravan Park (tel.: 01629 636302). Next door to Bakewell Camping and Caravanning Club Site. Same views and same location.

Left: Relaxing at the campsite in Youlgreave
Top Right: Pitches that make the most of the views
Bottom Right: The Peak District landscape in all its glory

Bank House Farm
Staffordshire

Any region that 'dresses' waterworks has got to be special. Either that or barking mad or looking for any excuse to throw a party. Well dressings are a traditional part of Peak District life, and though not exclusive to the area, they originated here several hundred years ago (around the time of the Black Death, it's believed) as a celebration to give thanks for the water of life. Many villages throughout the Peak District still dress the wells and springs with ornate pictures made from flowers, berries and other natural materials pressed into clay boards. Most well-dressing ceremonies take place throughout the summer months, at a time when camping also springs into action.

While these water sources are being dressed, you can run around in whatever state of dress takes your fancy (flowers obligatory in all the necessary places, though), right next to a watercourse at Bank House Farm, situated in the southern part of the Peak District. This campsite takes back to basics seriously: two large fields without electric hook-ups enforcing specific positions for pitches (though there are some with hook-ups if you need modern luxuries), so you select whichever bit of ground you like the look of and make your 'camp' – be it on top of the hill or down by the riverside; either way, there are great views of the hills around you. Some of the bank is too steep to pitch up on, or even mow, so it's just left wild, leaving the swaying grass and gorse bushes to do their own thing and allowing a few of nature's own to camp out too.

Depending on preference for hill or dale, 'vans can enter the site from two entrances, although it's recommended that larger 'vans stick to the flatter riverside area so that they don't get stuck when the ground gets soggy after prolonged rain. As if in a parkland setting, there's a large dwelling and a few old stone barns part way up the slope in a woodland garden; these house the reception, hot showers, toilets and, most importantly, the second-hand book-swap scheme for those who wish to thumb through a good selection of stories during their stay.

Above: Areas of the campsite are left wild to attract wildlife

The campsite is in the tiny village of Hulme End in the Staffordshire part of the Peak District. It's a whole lot quieter than the capers of the High Peak and, while there are still plenty of sharp ridges and incised valleys around to be inspired by, the countryside flattens out

Left: The Manifold Inn opposite Bank House Farm

from time to time too, making it easier on the calf muscles. The River Manifold runs through the site, which, although more than a bubbling brook, is neither the Nile in width or the Mississippi in length at just 12 miles long before it joins up with the neighbouring River Dove. Its name has been likened to 'many folds', owing to the excessive meandering that it manages to do within those 12 miles between its source, under the watchful gaze of Axe Edge near Buxton, and its marriage within the Ilam Estate. From the campsite you'd never know of its meandering, however, as there's not a bend in site, the river behaving impeccably straight as a rod, passing underneath the Hulme End bridge and away to meadows and turreting hills beyond. To experience its impetuous snake-like habit, you need to go for a wander, but that's only possible up to a point, as the river heads underground between Wetton Mill and Ilam. Instead, take the Manifold Way, an 8-mile track that begins at Hulme End, within a few yards of the campsite, and recycles an old, disused railway line that once trundled along to Waterhouses. The way is paved, making it accessible for wheelchairs as well as cyclists, and runs through some of the White Peak's prettiest limestone countryside, an area once favoured for copper mining and now popular with climbers who appear to hang like spiders on intricate silk threads.

For those preferring to hang on the words of an obliging waitress in a tea room, head to Hartington, a village 2 miles north of the campsite. It's one of those villages with a heart (and a village pond) that draws people (and ducks) to its centre; it's impossible to pass through without feeling either the need to stop and join in with the soothing pastime of people-watching over a cup of tea or an ever so slight resenting jealousy at those who are if you haven't got the time. For a restful state of mind, it's probably best to join them.

Bank House Farm

Hulme End, Hartington, Staffordshire, SK17 0EX

01298 84441

www.bankhousefarmcamping.co.uk

bankhousecampsite@gmail.com

Opening times: Beginning of March to end of October

Facilities: Hot showers, toilets, dishwashing, chemical toilet disposal point, recycling facilities, tumble dryer, gas sales, dog walk on separate field. Ramps and levellers required. Dogs welcome.

How to get there: From A515 Ashbourne to Buxton, turn onto B5054, signed Hartington. Continue through Hartington to Hulme End. Site entrance is at the bottom of hill almost directly opposite the Manifold Inn.

Food & drink: The Manifold Inn is directly opposite, with grounds for eating outdoors. An old coaching inn, it serves home-cooked food using local ingredients. The Devonshire Arms and Charles Cotton Hotel in Hartington are good too. Hulme End Stores sells everyday basics.

Nearby attractions: Hulme End is midway between the spa town of Buxton and Ashbourne, 'gateway to the peaks'. It's well Aplaced to explore Dove Dale as well as the Manifold valley; there's a visitor centre housed in the old railway station in the village. Ilam Park provides lots of walking at the other end of the River Manifold.

Alternative campsite: Hulme End Campsite (www.hulme-end-campsite.co.uk, tel.: 07800 659985). A basic site without hook-ups, behind the Manifold Inn on the opposite side of the road. Ramps and levellers required.

Top Left: Bridge over the River Manifold
Top Right: Bank House Farm
Bottom: Bank House Farm with views of the Staffordshire Peak District

Oaklea
Lincolnshire

There's no doubt that privately owned campsites take on the persona of the owners. And this campsite's owner, Piotr, is, quite simply, a lovely person – a gentle, laid-back and relaxed soul whose character and passion rub off on his garden site. Piotr created the garden site with his beloved wife, Pam, who sadly died in 2014. I met the lovely couple when preparing the first edition; her memory lives on in the beautiful gardens that she helped to create and loved so much, as Piotr continues to run the site.

Above: A caravan enjoying the space at Oaklea

For you are, literally, pitching in Piotr's garden – albeit a big garden, where there's no need to feel that you are intruding on the lodge-style house at the end of the drive, because there is plenty of room for all. That's because only five 'vans are allowed on site at any one time. This is what's known as a Certificated Location (CL), and as such you must be a member of the Caravan Club to be able to stay at Oaklea. But such is the beauty of the site and its location that it would be worth becoming a member simply to visit here alone.

Piotr and Pam had a passion, one that Piotr continues to be very happy to share with his guests – trees. Caravans pitch up in the 16-acre arboretum: a young, modern tree collection that the couple began planting in 1991. There are over 500 species planted, many of them rare. Ten acres are laid out to open grass, where much of the collection are planted sparsely, with magnificent views across the garden to specimen trees. Then there's 6 acres of open woodland with secret paths that disappear through the trees waiting to be explored. Guests staying on site are invited to wander around both the arboretum and the wood – a true privilege, as it's not open to the public. There are wooded glades, where the natural world of the denser woodland meets the garden with rhododendrons, camellias and briar roses adding a splash of colour to the woodland background. Piles of logs are stacked, waiting for winter and the wood-burning stove to kick into action.

Fritillaries, bluebells and primroses thrive in areas left wild and the sound of woodpeckers vibrates through the trees. Piotr described their mission, 'When we started the arboretum 25 years ago, we visited lots of stately homes and decided to create a new, modern Capability Brown-style parkland, but using all the trees from around the world that are available now, which of course he didn't have at his disposal.'

So the arboretum arrived first, the CL was created later and in 2006 it won the 'Best Newcomer' category in the

Right: Spring at Oaklea

Caravan Club's 'CL of the Year Awards'. Since then it has won many more awards, topped by winning the 'Most Picturesque CL' two years running. Oaklea only accepts adults, with the emphasis on peace and de-stressing in relaxed surroundings, so it provides the perfect excuse to leave the children with the grandparents and hop away for some me-time, and the perfect place for grandparents to make a dash to when they've handed back the little darlings. And because cars are only allowed on the grass to unhitch on arrival and are parked elsewhere for the remainder of the stay, the ground always looks good; no lumpy muddy patches or deep ruts.

To really fill the air with oxygen, the site backs onto 300 acres of Forestry Commission woodland – Ostler's Plantation and the 185-acre Kirkby Moor Nature Reserve (a Site of Special Scientific Interest) – so there are plenty of woodland walks. Just don't step on the sunbathing adders!

Oaklea is 1 mile from Woodhall Spa, a charming town to which the Victorians once flocked to take advantage of the mineral waters for curing ailments. Today, to cure stress, it's the heated outdoor swimming pool (summer months only) in the community-run Jubilee Park that allows you to lie back and watch the clouds float by. Woodhall Spa is also home to English Golf, which operates two spectacular courses at the National Golf Centre, open to day visitors. There's also the unique Kinema in the Woods, the only cinema in the country to use back projection.

Back at the campsite, if you hear the throaty sound of a Merlin engine, turn your head skyward. You may catch a glimpse of the Battle of Britain Memorial Flight, which resides at nearby RAF Coningsby and where there is a visitor centre and the chance to see the Lancaster, Spitfire and Hurricane aircraft up close.

Oaklea CL

Kirkby Lane, Kirkby-on-Bain, Woodhall Spa, Lincolnshire, LN10 6YY

01526 352352

www.oaklea.co.uk

pk@oaklea.co.uk

Opening times: Open all year

Facilities: Five pitches, hardstanding available, hook-ups, water point, chemical toilet disposal point. Dogs welcome. Adults only. Caravan Club members only – to become a member contact the Caravan Club (www.caravanclub.co.uk, tel.: 01342 318813).

How to get there: From the A17, turn onto the A153 to Coningsby. Turn left onto B1192, signed Woodhall Spa. In the village centre, turn right onto B1191, signed Horncastle. Just past the National Golf Centre, turn right into Kirkby Lane, signed Kirkby-on-Bain. The site is 1 mile farther on the left.

Food & drink: The Ebrington Arms, Kirkby-on-Bain is the village local with home-cooked food, real ales and a garden.

Nearby attractions: The cathedral city and county town of Lincoln is half an hour's drive, as are the beaches on the east coast. There are lots of historical RAF connections around the area, with several museums in the vicinity. The Lincolnshire Aviation Heritage Trail directs visitors to seven wartime airfields and operational stations. Tattershall Castle, a medieval red-brick castle owned by the National Trust, is a ten-minute drive away.

Alternative campsite: Woodhall Spa Camping and Caravanning Club Site (www.campingandcaravanningclub.co.uk, tel.: 01526 352911). A club site that is open to non-members, it is sited within the same woodlands that back onto Oaklea CL, with pitches among the trees.

Top: The 16 acres of ground at Oaklea
Bottom Left: Kinema in the Woods at Woodhall Spa
Bottom Right: Fritillaries thriving at the site

Fir Tree Farm
Warwickshire

You'll be hard-pressed to find anything coniferous at Fir Tree Farm Caravan Park, despite its name. For this is middle England and the landscapes around here are about as characteristic of English countryside as you're ever likely to see. Think gentle rolling hills made up of a collage of fields lined with ancient oaks, ash and hedgerows that would, once, have been crowned by the most handsome of English elm but instead are littered with the jewels of hawthorn rubies and the regal purple of plump blackberries.

Fir Tree Farm doesn't entirely perch on a hillside, more nuzzles into the last remaining folds (or first, depending on which way you look at it) of the most northerly Cotswold ridge, where the famous honey-coloured stone disappears and the rich, dark hues of ironstone take over.

Many of the touring pitches are tucked into the valley side, spaciously spread around an attractively landscaped half-acre fishing lake, with day tickets available for visitors. Every pitch has a decent view, but the higher up the valley slope you stay the better the unfolding panorama of the Sor Brook valley becomes. Indeed, you'll find Fir Tree Farm to be a split-level site: the lower of the two tiers is the more sheltered, while an upper terrace is more inclined to feel the wind when it blows – but pitches here are rewarded with by far the best views.

Though open enough to make the most of the scenery, the campsite is landscaped with the prettiest and most scented of wild rose screens among the pitches, pretty in pink all summer and dotted with striking walnut-sized hips in autumn. And, while sitting out to admire the view, there's every chance that you'll catch sight of a bird of prey for there's a falconry centre situated within the grounds of the campsite. There are 30 birds in all –falcons, hawks, buzzards and the most magnificent of owls – each one exercised on location. You can purchase vouchers for a falconry experience including photography days, 'hawk walks' and handling of the birds.

Above: Fir Tree Farm Caravan Park

Fir Tree Farm catches the sun all day and well into the evening so you're unlikely to want to leave, but you must, even if it's only on foot. For there are public footpaths in every direction, including the long-distance

Left: A caravan pitched at Fir Tree Farm

Macmillan Way passing half a mile north. A particularly good circular route that will encourage you to explore your nearest surroundings takes you across Sor Brook into neighbouring Oxfordshire (the stream provides the county boundary; confusingly the campsite attracts an Oxfordshire postal address while sited within Warwickshire), up and over Bush Hill, viewed from the campsite, to Hornton. This village provides the name for the local ironstone that's ever-present in these parts, and also offers the chance to step inside the George and Dragon for a refreshing taster of the local ale from nearby Hook Norton Brewery. From Hornton, it's a trek north to the oh-so-pictorial village of Ratley, tucked into the southern folds of Edge Hill before returning to the campsite via Warmington, utilising a small stretch of the Macmillan Way. In Warmington, you can always sit for a breather and a flask of tea beside the duck pond on the village green.

Edge Hill may sound familiar if you associate yourself with one or other of the Cavaliers and Roundheads. For the 1642 Battle of Edgehill is a notable mark in the calendar of the English Civil War. It divided local families, including those in villages like neighbouring Ratley. You can see the battlefield, now ironically covered by an ammunition store, from the top of Edge Hill. Every October, to mark the anniversary, a historical battle re-enactment takes place when pike men and musketeers draw arms once again.

Southeast of Edge Hill, and 5 miles or so from Fir Tree Farm, is Upton House. National Trust-owned, the country house displays an impressive art collection, including works by Canaletto and George Stubbs, though the gardens are no less remarkable with an impressive kitchen garden, bog garden and terraced borders.

Fir Tree Farm Caravan Park

Warmington, Banbury, Oxfordshire, OX17 1JL

07983 144681

www.firtreefalconry.co.uk

hawk@firtreefalconry.co.uk

Opening times: Open all year

Facilities: 35 pitches with hook-up, amenity building with toilets and showers, dishwashing, chemical toilet disposal point, fresh water, fishing lake (day tickets available), falconry experiences. Dogs welcome.

How to get there: From Banbury, take the B4100 north towards Warmington. In 3 miles, and 250 yards past the Falcon Inn, turn left onto the B4086, signposted Kineton. Site entrance immediately on left. Follow the track for ¼ mile to reception.

Food & drink: Both the Falcon Inn (tel.: 01295 692120) and National Herb Centre (café only) are within walking distance. The Plough Inn (tel.: 01295 690666) at Warmington offers good food as does the quirky Castle Inn at Edgehill, with fabulous views from the pub garden.

Nearby attractions: Besides those already mentioned, Fir Tree Farm is well situated for visits to Hook Norton Brewery Visitor Centre, Compton Verney (art gallery and 'Capability' Brown landscaped grounds), Silverstone race circuit, and, within a ½-hour drive, Bicester Village Outlet Shopping Centre.

Alternative campsite: The Pig Place (www.thepigplace.co.uk, tel.: 07892 879447). One mile south of Banbury and ¼ mile east of the village of Adderbury on B4100. A tiny caravan site on a working smallholding beside the Oxford Canal.

Top Left: A barn owl is just one of the many birds at Fir Tree Falconry
Top Right: Fishing at Fir Tree Farm
Bottom: The picturesque village of Warmington

Stratford Touring Park
Warwickshire

By all accounts, Stratford Touring Park would come under the ordinary category: a few rows of electric hook-ups in line-dancing fashion in a field with some pleasant campsite facilities. Nothing too remarkable about that, except for one thing – horses. Oh, and William Shakespeare. All right, that makes two things.

Above: Stratford Touring Park

The touring park is sited on Stratford Racecourse, one of the smaller, family-friendly horse-racing establishments that, throughout the summer, hosts several National Hunt (that's jumping over fences and hurdles, for the uninitiated) race meetings. Several racecourses around the UK house campsites, but most require campers to move their 'vans on race days. This is partly the case at Stratford; of the 50 pitches with hook-ups, 37 need to transfer to the centre of the course, which is no bad thing because you still get to

stay with your 'van and you can have a picnic or enjoy the Centre Course Enclosure facilities while watching the racing. However, there are 13 'premier' pitches, tucked up against a hedge for shelter, that are lined up for good reason – so all the visitors can stay with their 'vans, sit out on a picnic chair and watch the racing from the comfort of their pitch. We're not talking furlongs away either – the closest pitches to the track are no more than the height of a jockey.

There are freebies too, so it's odds-on a winner with any punter. Visitors to the campsite staying two nights or more receive two free tickets (children under 16 are free) to the Centre Course Enclosure. You'll have to stump up if you wish to join in with the canapés and bubbly in the glass-fronted grandstand or enjoy a meal in The Gallery Restaurant, but half the fun is creating your own gourmet lunch, served on a rug. Most race days involve fun-filled entertainment for the children (pack a flannel for when the face paint begins to wear thin) in addition to the permanent playground, which the youngsters can use on non-race days too.

The racecourse is bordered by the River Avon, and from the campsite there's a beautiful 15-minute walk along the riverbank to Stratford-upon-Avon's town centre. The route follows the Stratford Greenway nature trail through parkland, with one of the first buildings that you pass being Holy Trinity Church, Shakespeare's final resting place. The

Right: Pitches beside Stratford Racecourse

church sits in a quiet area of Stratford's Old Town and yet is a landmark, its tall spire rising heavenly beyond the rooftops.

Stratford-upon-Avon is a trap that snares tourists with its charm. It throbs with the movement of people the minute the sun peeps out, but this is understandable: quaint, photogenic, half-timbered houses, most of them appearing to be associated to any one of a number of Shakespeare's relatives; the river, busy with rowing boats for hire; the vast collection of restaurants, pubs and eateries; the Riverside Gardens, Recreation Ground (across the river), Canal Basin and the Bancroft Gardens, all suitable picnic territory or the place to brush up on some dramatic lines from the Bard. And then there are the theatres.

Shakespeare certainly does get everywhere, and his fame is milked for all it's worth; every few hundred yards around the town there's a reference to him or his plays – the name of a bed and breakfast, restaurant, museum or tour – nevertheless, visiting the theatre and listening to a few lines is inclined to make the hairs stand on end.

Home to the Royal Shakespeare Company (www.rsc.org.uk), which plays to packed houses most nights of the year, the theatres alternate the repertoire of the great man, selecting from his 38 plays, alongside those of his contemporaries and new writing from current playwrights. Even with sell-outs, some tickets are always sold on the day; there's usually a few returns, so queue up early for a chance to see that evening's show if your tickets haven't been pre-booked.

Farther afield, the Warwickshire countryside is spectacular. There are no mountains, no dramatic cliff tops or gorged valleys, just a gentle, undulating pastoral idyll that doesn't jar the senses.

Stratford Touring Park

Stratford Racecourse, Luddington Road,
Stratford-upon-Avon, Warwickshire, CV37 9SE

01789 201063

www.stratfordtouringpark.com

info@stratfordtouringpark.com

Opening times: Mid-March to end of October

Facilities: 80 level pitches with hook-ups (including 8 hard-standing), plus further non-electric pitches (mostly used for rallies), showers and toilet block, disabled facilities, laundry, chemical toilet disposal point, small playground, gas sales. Dogs welcome.

How to get there: Junction 15 off M40, A46 to Stratford, A4300 into town centre, B439, signed Bidford-on-Avon, out of town centre. Approximately 1 mile from the centre, turn left into Luddington Road. Site is 100 metres farther on the left.

Food & drink: Stratford-upon-Avon is filled with eating places of every type and price range but, for something a bit different, have a freshly prepared lunch or dinner on The Countess of Evesham while cruising the River Avon (www.countessofevesham.co.uk); bookings essential. For people-watching in a lively atmosphere, have a drink at The Dirty Duck on Waterside, just up from the theatre; it's not renowned for its food but it's where all the actors hang out after a show.

Nearby attractions: For racing at Stratford and a list of race days, see www.stratfordracecourse.net. Charlecote Park, 5 miles from Stratford, is where the young William allegedly went poaching for deer; the ancestral beasts are still there, so he obviously didn't poach them all. You can wander the park's grounds – the Avon meanders through the middle – and visit the imposing brick Tudor house.

Alternative campsite: Riverside Caravan Park (www.stratfordcaravans.co.uk, tel.: 01789 292312). On the banks of the River Avon, a straightforward site with a mixture of tourers, seasonal caravans and static holiday homes. Some touring pitches have river views.

Top Left: The River Avon
Top Right: Anne Hathaway's cottage in Stratford-upon-Avon, where William Shakespeare wooed his future wife
Bottom: Stratford Racecourse

Monaughty Poeth
Shropshire

If the campsite at Monaughty Poeth were just ten paces farther away, across the bridge and over the river, then it would not make it into this guide to England's caravan sites. That's not to say that the views are suddenly awful; on the contrary, it would be hard to find such a beautiful location for a campsite. It's simply that the Welsh border runs along the side; actually, it rushes rather than runs, as the swift flowing waters of the River Teme stumble over shallow rocks and shingle to carve its way between the Welsh and English countryside.

Above: The England/Wales border – The River Teme

Monaughty Poeth is a sheep farm and has been for generations. 'Monaughty' translates to 'Monastery Grange' and in the 12th century it produced the food for the monks at a local abbey. It's had a disastrous life, though (the 'Poeth' part of its name means 'burned'), as the grange has suffered many fires over the centuries,

with the chimney stack, ironically enough, being all that's left of the original building.

It's now home to Jim and Jocelyn Williams – true country people who care deeply for their land and look forward to visitors enjoying it with them. Although Jim has scaled down his flock of sheep in later years, he can still be seen shepherding the woolly bleaters assisted by his beloved sheepdogs, a symbol to the traditional way of life around these border villages.

Half of their farm is in Wales, the remainder, including the farmhouse, barns and campsite are in England, a true border post. People have fought over this soil for years, the land toing and froing between raging factions several times. Then, some chap called Offa, King of Mercia way back in the late 18th century, built (or at least rallied a band of men with shovels) a dyke that served both as a territorial boundary and a defence between his land and Wales. The 80-mile long, 26-foot high bank runs from Wrexham to Chepstow, and the associated National Trail, Offa's Dyke Path, runs adjacent to the farm.

The land around the campsite is a geologist's dream. For mortals who simply like something good to look at and a spot of peace, it's also utter heaven. If there's a site that epitomizes 'cool' locations, this has to be it. Think the lower peaks of the Lake District without the lakes … oh, and without the hordes. It's a forgotten

Right: The River Teme, running past the campsite

land, the last outpost in England where you can feel space, where you can still wander the country lanes peacefully – just occasionally needing to stand among the campion and cow parsley on the verge for a passing tractor or a working sheepdog – and where the dichotomy of the hills and valleys are as idyllic to gaze at in winter – the skeletal trees silhouetted against a hillside – as they are in any other season.

Relaxing on the campsite, a Caravan Club Certificated Location that only accepts five 'vans at a time, is more laid back than a tune from Barry White. With so few vehicles on the one-acre plot, it's never crowded and everyone gets a view up and down the valley, as well as of the river with its tiny stone bridge and the hills to either side that rise gently against the horizon. Combine the views with the soft song of the river and the sheep's call, and any shoulder-hunching stress that you left home or work with will be eradicated within minutes. The only thing left to concern yourself with is which way to walk first – along the land towards Graig Wood for a spectacular hazy embankment of bluebells, or nipping into Wales for a riverside wander to skim the slate shale stones over the surface and peer for trout.

Knighton, the closest town over the border, houses the Offa's Dyke Centre where there's more information about the king and his dyke. Uniquely, too, Knighton's Spaceguard Centre is the only place in the UK studying the threat that comets and asteroids pose to the Earth. If you're confident that the world won't come to an end during your stay, Clun, 7 miles north of Knighton and back in England, has a fine, if derelict, castle; one of the many fortifications from more turbulent times in the border counties. More recently, the town hosts the Clun Green Man Festival celebrating the arrival of spring. So, you can ponder the destruction of the universe and rejoice the rites of spring all within a few miles of each other – it sounds almost biblical.

Monaughty Poeth

Llanfair Waterdine, Knighton, Shropshire, LD7 1TT

01547 528348

Opening times: Open all year

Facilities: Five pitches with hook-ups, chemical toilet disposal point, rubbish disposal, trout fishing. Dogs welcome on leads.

How to get there: A49 Hereford to Shrewsbury, turn onto A4113 at Bromfield, in Knighton turn right onto B4355, signed Newtown, take first right just past Knucklas bypass. The site is 300 metres farther on the left, immediately after river bridge.

Food & drink: The Waterdine (www.waterdine.com, tel.: 01547 528214) serves good food using local ingredients and cooked by a renowned Master Chef, but is quite pricey. Bookings only.

Nearby attractions: Follow Offa's Dyke Path or, for a change, Glyndwr's Way in Wales. The ruined castle at Clun is atmospheric, while a little farther afield is Stokesay Castle.

Alternative campsite: Clun Valley Camping (www.clunvalleycamping.co.uk, tel.: 01588 640041) in Newcastle, one valley farther north and on Offa's Dyke Path.

Left: The River Teme by the site
Top Right: Bluebells at Graig Wood
Bottom Right: Monaughty Poeth is a working sheep farm

Whitcliffe Campsite
Shropshire

If you attempt to eat a cereal bar while rushing through Ludlow's Market Square with a mobile pressed to your ear, the chances are you might find frowns adorning the face of a more relaxed Salopian. For medieval Ludlow is the birthplace of the Slow Food UK movement; its HQ was in the town until 2009, when it moved to London to seek a higher profile among the political powers that be; although slow food in Ludlow is more about cheeseboards with a regional flavour than high-pressured board meetings.

Unsurprisingly, there's a very strong emphasis on slow food within the town, where restaurants and gastro-pubs use seasonal ingredients from the fields virtually in sight, and it's hoped that households will do the same, supporting the nearby farms, butchers, bakers and suppliers, thereby saving traditional fare from the onslaught of the institutional burger. The town's autumn food festival is renowned throughout Britain as being one of the must-visit shows.

Ludlow was the first Cittàslow – or Slow Town – in Britain, where whole communities work towards a better quality of life for all residents and visitors, and where the town has an independent identity, rather than a cloned high street looking much like any other. The town is no longer affiliated to the organisation but, wandering around (at a snail's pace, naturally), most retailers are still independent, many sited in the 500 or so listed buildings in the town.

But those slow eaters residing in the half-timbered houses in the town centre don't have the benefits afforded to visitors at Whitcliffe Campsite, where you can while away the hours at tortoise speed on a grassy bank. It has a view to surpass all others of Ludlow, with the Norman castle and the tower of St Laurence's Parish Church looking close enough to touch.

Above: A tasty selection of breads at Ludlow Food Centre

The walk into town is a very pleasant 1-mile trek downhill across Whitcliffe Common, and deposits you by the castle walls alongside the River Teme; just don't forget that there will be a mile of puffing, panting and pulling of calf muscles on the return.

The 12 pitches for caravans and motorhomes – all with hook-ups – are terraced so that nobody spoils anyone else's view and everyone gets a level spot. But the

views don't end at the town boundaries. The site has a scenic backcloth of Titterstone Clee Hill and Brown Clee Hill; these are two of Shropshire's highest points, squeezed upwards by geological activity, true to Ludlow form, very slowly rather a long time ago. The sun slowly peeks its early morning face from behind these hills, illuminating the remainder of the stage set in the wings – to the left, views of the north Shropshire hills, where further geological rumblings once occurred when woolly mammoths trod the earth; to the right, the Arcadian pastures of Herefordshire, glistening with its orchards of rosy fruit.

Facilities, at the back of the campsite (so it's an uphill trek for those on the lower slopes of the bank), are basic but functional and clean. There are two showers and toilets, indoor washing-up facilities, power points and a chemical toilet disposal point that, thoughtfully for other campers, is discreetly hidden behind a screen away from the main field.

Whitcliffe continues the slow theme, encouraging visitors into Mortimer Forest next door on horseback or on foot. With a riding school on site, the horses live in the fields around the campers. Experienced riders and novices of all ages can take to the saddle for a slow trot through the forest, away from busy roads. Children take control for themselves, with instruction rather than being rein-led, with rides of up to two hours. Alternatively, children can spend a full instructional day at the riding school, leaving parents free to make the most of some slow time, perhaps for a saunter to the brewery, the Ludlow Brewing Co., with a visitor centre and on-site bar. Gary Walters, the owner, will show you around and you can taste a drop of whatever's on brew, but the idea is to buy a bottle or two for later consumption – all in the name of supporting the local, of course; in truth, you'll need it once you've climbed back up to the campsite.

Whitcliffe Campsite

North Farm, Whitcliffe, Ludlow, Shropshire, SY8 2HD

01584 872026

www.northfarmludlow.co.uk

info@northfarmludlow.co.uk

Opening times: April to the end of September

Facilities: 12 pitches with hook-ups, free hot showers, three toilets, dishwashing, shaver/power points, chemical toilet disposal point. Dogs welcome, horse riding on site.

How to get there: From the A49, turn onto the B4361 to Ludlow. From the town centre, cross over the river bridge and turn immediately right, signed Whitcliffe. The entrance to the site is half a mile up the hill on the left.

Food & drink: The Ludlow Food Centre (www.ludlowfoodcentre.co.uk) is 1 mile out of Ludlow on the A49 towards Shrewsbury – an impressive farm shop-style building selling local everything and where you can watch the artisan producers making goodies in the show kitchens. There's a restaurant on site, too, serving seasonal fare.

Nearby attractions: Visit the castle ramparts or go shopping in Ludlow, where there are lots of interior design and period house accessory shops. Craven Arms, Church Stretton and Cleobury Mortimer are all within 20 minutes' drive of Ludlow. Or take a walk on Clee Hill for a several-county view.

Alternative campsite: Westbrook Park (www.westbrookpark.co.uk, tel.: 01584 711280). Located in an old orchard by the banks of the River Teme in Little Hereford, 6 miles from Ludlow. Some road noise from the A456.

Top: Views of Shropshire from Whitcliffe Campsite
Bottom Left: Rhododendrons at Whitcliffe Campsite
Bottom Right: Horseriding is possible from the campsite

Rowlestone Court
Herefordshire

Think Herefordshire and many tend to conjure up images of monochrome timber-framed houses, apples and cider, while those unfamiliar with the county attempt a 'country' accent unheard in any shire and cry, 'Oooh, Ahhh'. Well, Mark and Mary Williams have added a new dimension to the county and it doesn't involve pressing apples or silly voices, though black and white does come into it. What happens is this: a herd of Friesian dairy cows (they're the black and white ones) are put out to eat the rich and luscious pastures around Rowlestone Court Farm, admiring the views of the Welsh Hills as they chew their food. Mark collects his girls morning and evening from the fields and escorts them to the milking parlour, where they deliver their delicious creamy milk, ready to be pasteurized. The cows are returned to the pastures and Mary comes along to collect the milk and cream, which she makes into even more delicious and moreishly tasty ice cream, sold in the cafe on the farm. So, customers can see the very cows that supplied the milk for their dessert, talk to the very farmer who milked them and select the finest flavour from the lady who makes it. Every part of the process is performed on the farm with no food miles.

Agricultural diversification can be a dirty word in farming, as it can hide the truth, which is that some farms are being forced to stop farming and farmers have to stop doing what they do best – producing food. Thankfully, at Rowlestone Court, that's not the case;

diversifying into artisan ice-cream making has simply brought the farm's produce back home. Thankfully, too, for all of us, the Williams have opened up their farm, allowing campers to share the beauty of their patch. And it's a patch worth visiting, both to sample a cornet with a little ball of heaven on top and to enjoy views that would warm the hearts of any ice-cold soul.

Above: Rowlestone Court

From the gently sloping open field, there's a 360-degree panorama that looks out across Herefordshire and the Black Mountains in Wales. You really are away from it all at Rowlestone Court, the nearest village (Rowlestone, as luck would have it for remembering names) and main road are more than a mile away, with dense woods in between. The nearest towns, Abergavenny in Wales and Hereford, are both a whopping 12 miles away in differing directions. That's not to say that the site, or

Left: Looking towards Wales from the wildlife pond at Rowlestone Court

the farm, is not civilized. On the contrary, it's the perfect place for civility, to chill out on the multi-award-winning ice creams, to drink in the solitude, to appreciate the agricultural surroundings and to understand what it's like to live in the middle of a field.

The recently refurbished campsite facilities are first-rate, with baby-changing rooms and family-sized showers. To stay at an ice-cream farm is, after all, a child's idea of paradise, where the challenge of your stay is to try every flavour. With over 40 flavours to choose from, that's no mean feat. The fenced-off playground is not your ordinary run-of-the-mill equipment either. There's a big red tractor for imagining life ploughing the fields and a series of secret dens carefully woven from living willow in which to escape the parents.

When you feel the need to walk off the ice cream, don a pair of boots and head for the series of wildlife gardens and ponds (with impaired-mobility access), where kids of all ages can fill a jam jar with scientific specimens for closer inspection. Farther up the field, two saddleback pigs wallow in 'Piggy's Paradise', sunbathing under the coolness of the Colony Wood. The wild-flower meadow will, without doubt, take your eye off the views in summer, when a mixture of native plants bask in the sunshine opening their petals to make themselves attractive to the indigenous population of butterflies and bees.

By the time you reach the Woodland Adventure Trail, with substantial climbing frame made from sweet chestnut and large, cantilevered tyre swing for the energetic, and the old lime kilns in the far-off trees, it will be time to make a quick U-turn and start pondering which flavour you'll try next on arrival back at the campsite. So, to whet your appetite … there's Caramel, Forest Fruits, Vanilla, Honeycomb, Hazelnut, Ginger, Mango Sorbet, Strawberry Sorbet …Yum.

Rowlestone Court

Rowlestone, Herefordshire, HR2 0DW

01981 240322

www.rowlestonecourt.co.uk

info@rowlestonecourt.co.uk

Opening times: April to October

Facilities: Five pitches all with hook-ups (Rowlestone Court is a Certificated Site, so you must be a member of The Camping and Caravanning Club to stay, although you can become a member on site), toilets, free hot showers, family shower room, disabled facilities, dishwashing, play area, woodland walks. Dogs welcome.

How to get there: A465 Hereford to Abergavenny road, turn off in Pontrilas, signposted for Rowlestone. Site is the second farm on the right after 1½ miles – narrow lane.

Food & drink: Eat on site; the cafe serves hot and cold drinks all day as well as delicious home-made quiche and salads, lunchtime snacks, home-made cakes and scones, plus ice cream!

Nearby attractions: Take a cycling/driving tour along Golden valley for some spectacularly beautiful countryside. Wales is 3 miles away, with the Black Mountains for great walking territory.

Alternative campsite: Burhope Farm Campsite (www.burhope farmcampsite.co.uk, tel.: 01981 580275). Open field-based site in Orcop surrounded by spectacular, peaceful Herefordshire countryside.

Top: Friesian cows supply the milk for the ice cream
Bottom Left: Play equipment is unconventional
Bottom Right: The farm's delicious ice cream

Hayles Fruit Farm
Gloucestershire

Food, glorious food. There can't be a person in the land who doesn't enjoy crouching between rows of beckoning strawberries. Who can resist the temptation to nibble when the berries, peeking through the leaves, encourage dribbling and drooling as the punnet begins to fill and the scent of sunshine strikes the nose. There's no doubt about it, nature designed its packaging just right to make us mortals sway to the seduction of a strawberry.

Above: The campsite at Hayles Fruit Farm

So a campsite on a pick-your-own fruit farm is a foodie's dream. Add to that some glorious views of the Cotswold countryside and you've a recipe that will leave anyone foraging for more.

Hayles Fruit Farm has been in the Harrell family for donkey's years. They've got a nice little spot down a road that goes nowhere other than their own farm, and you'll probably see one of the family members either on the tractor, checking the fruit trees or serving the customers in the on-site farm shop. Behind the farm is quite a well-known landmark, Salter's Hill, one of those hills that defines the Cotswolds – steep, but not too steep. There's a single-track road that winds its way up the hill and from which you can look down onto the farm and the campsite. The hill top, so named because of the ancient Salt Way (transporting salt from the Midlands to London) crossing it, commands a good view and, if your calf muscles will allow you to reach the summit, a mere 263 metres above sea level, it will supply you with some impressive panoramas of other Cotswold hills and the Vale of Evesham. It's all very pretty and you begin to understand why visitors from across the pond come in their droves to share this particular part of England.

The campsite is, put simply, just a field; unpretentious, with a few hook-ups and some hardstanding pitches arranged in a ring. It too has good views from all angles of the various hills (including Salter's), agricultural land and Hailes Wood, which adjoins the farm. Yet the site still manages to retain some traditional Cotswold hedges that keep it sheltered and private. There are fruit trees that stretch almost as far as one can see, an absolute treat if you happen to catch the spring blossom. The no-through road (the only traffic going to and from the farm) makes it blissfully peaceful and a very pleasant

Right: Hailes Abbey

spot to spend a weekend. In the evening you can gaze into the glowing embers of a campfire, while fighting over the last strawberry.

If there's a downside, there is only one shower and loo per girl and boy, housed in an ageing Portakabin, which struggles to cope on busy days. Those preferring the finer comforts should stick with their on-board facilities.

But what the Portakabin lacks – that can easily be overcome – the rest of the farm makes up for. The farm shop stocks all that you'd hope for in local produce, including seasonal fruit from the surrounding fields and apple juice and cider made from their own harvest – about eight different varieties to get squiffy on. There's a large coarse-fishing lake with day tickets available; campers can pay by the hour if you fancy a dabble just for the evening.

In the neighbouring field the ruined remains of Hailes Abbey lay peacefully under the chestnut trees, a once important site that attracted thousands of pilgrims to wonder and revere the phial of Christ's blood that was, allegedly, held there. From here, the Cotswold Way takes walkers into Winchcombe, a town that looks as if it grew from the soil, made with the subtle creamy yellow tones of the local stone. King Offa made Winchcombe the capital of his Kingdom of Mercia and therefore the most important town in the Cotswolds. Now the area's importance lies in the pilgrims who flock to revere the architecture and hyphenated beauties, such as Stow-on-the-Wold, Moreton-in-Marsh and Bourton-on-the-Water.

One other architectural gem, around the other side of Salter's Hill, is Sudeley Castle. This significant structure, with many historical royal connections, blends into the local landscape and its architecture and gardens have to be on the 'must visit' list.

Hayles Fruit Farm

Winchcombe, Gloucestershire, GL54 5PB

01242 602123

www.haylesfruitfarm.co.uk

info@haylesfruitfarm.co.uk

Opening times: Open all year

Facilities: 12 hardstanding pitches with hook-ups, basic/limited showers/loos, chemical toilet disposal, good farm shop and cafe on the farm (50 metres from the campsite), fishing lakes. Campfires allowed in fire pits provided.

How to get there: Junction 9 on M5, A46, signed Evesham. At first roundabout follow B4077 towards Stow-on-the-Wold. At Toddington, turn right onto B4632 towards Winchcombe. In 2 miles turn left signed Hayles Fruit Farm and Hailes Abbey. Follow signs for Hailes Abbey (half a mile from road). Campsite is just past abbey grounds.

Food & drink: The Lion Inn in Winchcombe (www.thelion winchcombe.co.uk, tel.: 01242 603300) is a 15th-century coaching inn serving excellent British food using local ingredients.

Nearby attractions: The Gloucestershire & Warwickshire Steam Railway runs occasional old-fashioned trips from Toddington to Cheltenham. Snowshill Manor and village is 5 miles from the campsite. The spa town of Cheltenham is also 5 miles away.

Alternative campsite: Cotswold Farm Park (www.cotswoldfarmpark.co.uk, tel.: 01451 850307). Home to BBC Countryfile presenter Adam Henson, this is the farm park specializing in domestic rare breeds that his father set up in the seventies. The caravan park has lovely views across the Cotswolds.

Left: Apple blossoms at Hayles Fruit Farm
Top Right: The Cotswold town of Winchcombe
Bottom Right: Apples grown at Hayles Fruit Farm

South-East

Sandringham
Norfolk

Staying at Her Majesty's pleasure is not a holiday most would wish for, but staying for *your* pleasure at Her Majesty's country retreat could be considered a more palatable option, especially if you can temporarily call The Queen your neighbour.

Sandringham is the privately owned estate of the Royal Family. It's where they hang up stockings and wait for Father Christmas to pick a chimney (there are several on the house) during the festive time and hibernate from the media scrum over winter.

The vast estate is run along traditional lines, working with the seasons, with arable farming at its heart. A working sawmill makes fencing and gates for the local community and sells firewood and Christmas trees during the winter. It plants more than 5,000 trees each year. The estate is also home to the Royal Fruit Farm, which turns the apples from the orchard planted by King George V into juice that's served at royal garden parties and receptions, or you can buy it in the estate's visitor centre. The fruit farm also grows organic blackcurrants for Ribena and is experimenting with an organic black truffle plantation. Fruit and vegetables grown in the old Walled Garden are also used in the visitor centre restaurant.

Close to the north-west coast of Norfolk, just before the land falls into The Wash, the house and 60-acre gardens are, for a fee, open to visitors when the Royals are elsewhere. However, the general public has free access to much of the 600-acre wooded Country Park that surrounds the residence. The park is renowned for its late spring show of shocking pink, when rhododendrons and azaleas strike hard against the slow-performing leaflets of lazier trees and shrubs, kick-starting summer with a bang. It's a great spot for a woodland picnic or good old-fashioned autumn stomp on crunchy leaves frosted to the earth too.

Above: Wood pigeon on the Sandringham estate

Less than a mile from the Royal Christmas retreat, and within the Country Park is the Camping and Caravanning Club's campsite, but you don't have to be a member of the club to stay here. The campsite may not offer the opulence of a royal palace, but it does provide a secure woodland setting with modern facilities that are very well maintained. It's a large site that can get very busy, but each woodland glade is split into

---

Top Left: The tall trees of Sandringham Camping and Caravanning Club Site **Bottom Left:** Pine cones on the campsite ground

enclosures separated by the tall pine trees and silver birch, so that the site feels less daunting than it actually is. It's totally surrounded, too, by more firs and birch, giving the site a Scandinavian feel and complete seclusion; yet, because of the open spaces, where the dappled sun glows through the spindly tree trunks, it's by no means gloomy, with plenty of rabbits and birdsong to listen out for. Pooches will love the walks in the woods around the perimeter of the site, with longer hikes throughout the rest of the estate. All the pitches are on the mostly level grass, serviced by hardstanding roads. You may choose your own pitch, with or without hook-up, on arrival, with the quieter areas tending to be at the far ends of the site, farthest away from the amenity blocks. Wi-fi is available.

Off-site the long stretch of sandy beach along the North Norfolk coast begins 5 miles away. There's an RSPB nature reserve at Snettisham, while the traditional seaside resort of Hunstanton will take you back to childhood holidays by the beach. There's a string of other coastal villages that run along the coastline too – Brancaster, Burnham Market and Holkham.

Ten miles north of Sandringham is Norfolk Lavender, home to the National Lavender Collection, where the air is fragranced by a heady scent of perfume and the hazy violet hues of lavender grace the fields Provençal-style. You can tour the purple fields or breathe in the wafting aromas in the distillery on summer days, with plenty more to look at during other times of the year.

Close to Fakenham, and 20 miles from the campsite, is Pensthorpe Nature Reserve. It's open all year round with lots to see and do in any season, whether its pond dipping in spring or watching the visiting geese prepare for winter.

Sandringham Camping and Caravanning Club Site

The Sandringham Estate, Double Lodges, Sandringham, Norfolk, PE35 6EA

01485 542555

www.campingandcaravanningclub.co.uk

Opening times: mid-February to beginning of January

Facilities: 275 grass pitches, hook-ups, motorhome service point, hot showers, parent-and-baby room, family shower room, disabled facilities, laundry, dishwashing, playground, shop, gas exchange, wi-fi access. Dogs welcome.

How to get there: A149 from Kings Lynn, then A148 towards Fakenham. Turn left onto B1440 and left again onto B1439. Through West Newton, turn right at brown campsite signpost and follow campsite signs through the estate.

Food & drink: The Sandringham Estate Visitor Centre includes a restaurant and coffee shop, often using estate produce. The Pick Your Own Apples season on the Sandringham Estate runs from September to October.

Nearby attractions: The Peddars Way and the Norfolk Coast Path run close by to the estate. The Green Britain Centre at Swaffham provides tours of the wind turbine and there's plenty of culture at Houghton Hall, Oxburgh Hall and the Holkham Estate.

Alternative campsite: Sandringham Estate Caravan Club Site (www.caravanclub.co.uk, tel.: 01553 631614). Not to be confused with the Camping and Caravanning Club, the Caravan Club has a site virtually next door that's open to non-members. It is a much more open campsite with less shade.

Top Left: The campsite, sitting in the wooded estate
Bottom Left: The gates to Sandringham House
Right: Sandringham Country Park

Willowcroft
Norfolk

Willowcroft has an enviable location: tucked secretively near the end of a tiny dead-end road where the sound of silence overtakes the noise of traffic. If you're in need to hear anything other than the dropping of a pin on the grass, cast your ear skyward and you might hear the gliding whoosh of a swan's wingbeat overhead, for Willowcroft is within a minute's walk – at the most – of the River Thurne, one of the waterways that meander through the upper reaches of the Norfolk Broads.

Above: Boat on the River Thurne

It's a quiet, unpretentious site owned by James and Kandy Trigg-Dudley, who live in the house opposite. They bought it over 20 years ago and have revamped the few facilities over the years, but the site has been a part of the community for almost 50 years, when it was really just a farmer's field. To some extent, that's what it still is – a manicured field with 30 pitches

marked out by baby corner hedges, and a mixture of young and mature trees. Around the edges of the field are the willows that give the site its name, carefully pollarded and well manicured like the rest. A band of more mature trees shelters the east side of the campsite. Beyond lies open farmland, with views across to the river.

As a tiny uncommercial site, the facilities are limited to necessities – water, waste disposal and heated toilets and showers in a small timber building that you hardly notice is there. No gimmicks, no bars and restaurants, no entertainment other than that you make yourself. And being in the Broads, there's plenty to do.

Kandy and James are a friendly couple. They'll chat willingly to those that fancy a natter about the local area and try to be on-call as much as they can if you need a hand. Likewise, if you want to be left alone, they won't be calling by every waking moment to disturb the peacefulness of the site. The village of Repps is a close-knit community with lots of activities going on throughout the year, and visitors staying at Willowcroft are warmly welcomed to the various functions, whether it's the charitable summer fête, the harvest festival, a Repps Revellers theatre production or one of the summer barbecues held at the Wind Energy Museum near the campsite. Willowcroft is all about community spirit and bringing people together.

Right: Willowcroft

With the river so close to the site, it's impossible to stay without paying it a visit. There are footpaths that run alongside, with quaint timber lodges and cottages on the water's edge. As the most important wetland area in Britain, with National Park status, the Broads are full of wildlife, so it's inevitable that you'll see as many birds as you will boats. Newts and lizards also enjoy the marshy areas around the Thurne, so watch where you're treading.

With the river in front of you, if you walk left along the bank, it's a 45-minute walk to the village of Thurne – use the village windmill as a landmark – which has a pub, The Lion Inn, to stop for a drink before the return journey. Walking right takes you on the 20-minute trek to Potter Heigham, one of the main places on the Broads, next to the bridge, for hopping onto the water. Broads Tours (www.broadstour.co.uk, tel.: 01603 782207) hire out self-drive boats (by the hour, half-day or full day), with instruction given before venturing off alone, or, for those who prefer to leave the work to someone else, they have a fleet of British-built cruisers that give guided river tours.

For a truly unique experience it's possible to charter one of the traditional Norfolk wherries, Albion (www.wherryalbion.com), that still cruises the Broads (this needs to be planned in advance). Originally used to carry cargo, these amazingly beautiful sailing boats have a charismatic charm. The Albion is moored at Ludham, and can accommodate 12 (plus skipper and mate), so put a group together for a special time.

Sticking to the Thurne, angling is free along the riverbank and there are fishing platforms for wheelchair users on the south bank, upstream of New Bridge at Potter Heigham, with access along the boardwalk from the campsite.

Willowcroft Camping and Caravan Park

Staithe Road, Repps-with-Bastwick,
Potter Heigham, Norfolk, NR29 5JU

01692 670380

www.willowcroft.net

willowcroftsite@btinternet.com

Opening times: March to October

Facilities: 30 pitches (including hardstanding), hook-ups, hot showers and toilets in heated amenity building, dishwashing, chemical toilet disposal point. Dogs welcome.

How to get there: A47 Norwich to Great Yarmouth road, at Acle, turn left onto A1064, turn left, signed Repps-with-Bastwick. In the village, turn left at sign for the campsite. Just past Manor Farm, turn right at T-junction into Staithe Road. Site is quarter of a mile farther on the right.

Food & drink: You'll be hard-pressed to find upmarket gastro-pubs in the immediate vicinity. The Lion Inn, Thurne (www.lion-inn-thurne.co.uk, tel.; 01692 670796) has a basic menu and a riverside garden but doesn't have the greatest reputation for its food. Stick with a drink and enjoy the location. The Falgate Inn (tel.: 01692 670003) at Potter Heigham serves straight-forward pub grub too. A trip to Norwich is necessary for a selection of great places to eat.

Nearby attractions: The golden beaches of the Norfolk coast are a matter of minutes' drive away. Norwich is a half-hour drive; its magnificent cathedral is well worth a look, as are the narrow streets of the medieval old town. The campsite is well placed to visit some of the other Broads, such as Hickling, Barton and Ormesby. For an old-fashioned seaside resort, Cromer is 24 miles away on the north coast.

Alternative campsite: Clippesby Hall (www.clippesbyhall.com, tel.: 01493 367800). A large site with an intimate, friendly feel and lots of facilities, including its own pub.

Top: The River Thurne
Bottom Left: A caravan at Willowcroft
Bottom Right: A mallard enjoying the river

The Dower House
Norfolk

Sometimes it's evident that you're arriving somewhere special. Turning off from the A1066, you first drive along a road so ruler-straight that an artist's perspective brings the road to a narrowing pinprick, all the while slicing through the trees. Then, turning off down a bumpy forest track, there's no sign of human life; the track simply keeps going on and on. Then, finally, the track turns and through the trees is the first glimpse of a caravan. Suddenly, after all those minutes under the canopy, there's a large open glade, in the middle of which stands the beautifully proportioned red-brick Dower House, an 18th-century husband's bequest to his wife.

Above: The Dower House

If there's ever a promise that can be kept, it's that visitors staying at The Dower House will not hear road noise. Here, you literally are in the thick of it. The 20-acre site, deep in Thetford Forest, is enclosed by hundreds of acres of mature mixed woodland, where guests can frolic beneath the trees and become acquainted with deer, foxes and maybe the odd badger on a late-night foraging mission.

There's nothing too formal about the pitches – they're marked out by strips of mown grass and radiate out from the large focal play area; it's like a good old-fashioned village green ready for a spot of cricket overseen by the umpiring grandfather, the old oak tree. The most popular pitches are those closest to the playground, where there's not so much shade from the midday sun. For campers who prefer solitude and a little extra privacy there's plenty of space to creep to the perimeter and find a shady hidey-hole under the trees; just don't anticipate a hook-up in the farther reaches of the park. There are five pitches specially designed for disabled campers sited close to the top-notch facilities, which include an adapted washroom.

Summer visitors can make a splash in the two outdoor swimming pools next to the house, with one especially for the very youngest family members. You'll certainly want to dip a toe into these, especially after a casual walk in the campsite's new nature trails through a wetland area – teeming with wildflowers and wildlife.

Behind the house you can sup a relaxing drink in The Travellers Rest, the on-site watering hole designed as an old-country family inn and cafe rather than a

Right: Thorpe Woodlands surrounding the campsite

boozer, with a roaring fire for chilly autumn evenings or parasols to keep the summer rays off in the garden.

With the trees so close by, children can romp around the forest to their heart's content, and when exploration takes you farther afield, there are footpaths and cycle tracks to unlock the mysteries of the woods, whether it be rooting for acorns before the squirrels horde them or establishing which trees spring into leaf first. The campsite should be able to help with tree and animal identification – having been awarded the David Bellamy Gold Conservation Award for 15 consecutive years, they have many attributes for encouraging wildlife.

The Dower House is well located to visit any number of Norfolk attractions. The main area of Thetford Forest (the campsite is in Thorpe Woodlands, a section that's broken ranks) has lots more walking and cycling where pines take precedent over their deciduous friends. If the feet are pleading to stop, let the children break free and head for the High Lodge Forest Centre to explore the play area or, for adrenalin-pumping stuff, zip off to the Go Ape high-wire forest adventure.

For something altogether more relaxing, the Bressingham Gardens are a short drive from the site. Renowned the world over, they were created by father-and-son team Alan and Adrian Bloom and you can take away samples of your day's visit.

And for those who fancy a tipple, take a trip to the neighbouring village of Roudham. One of only a handful of whisky makers in England, St George's Distillery is housed in a beautiful, traditional East Anglian timber-framed building where you can see the copper pipes and bulbs working away through giant glass windows. Established in 2006, you can take a tour of the distillery before sampling a couple of the malts.

The Dower House Touring Park

Thetford Forest, East Harling, Norfolk, NR16 2SE

01953 717314

www.dowerhouse.co.uk

info@dowerhouse.co.uk

Opening times: End of March to beginning of October

Facilities: Grass pitches with and without hook-ups, pitches for disabled campers, clean shower and toilet blocks, baby wash/changing room, disabled facilities, chemical toilet disposal point, dishwashing, laundry, shop, swimming and splash pools, playground, bar and cafe area. Dogs welcome.

How to get there: A11 Newmarket to Norwich road. Turn onto A1066 at Thetford, signed for Diss. Just past the village of Shadwell, turn left signed for East Harling. After approximately 2 miles, turn left at signpost for The Dower House. Follow the track through the woods until you reach the site.

Food & drink: The English Whisky Co. (www.englishwhisky.co.uk) in Roudham provides tastings of their various liquors and runs a small cafe with sandwiches and homemade cakes on site.

Nearby attractions: Discover life in the world of the Anglo-Saxons in the reconstructed village at West Stow Country Park, approximately 12 miles from the campsite; Banham Zoo is 5 miles away; or head underground to visit one of the Neolithic shafts 9 metres below ground level at Grime's Graves.

Alternative campsite: Brick Kiln Farm (www.norfolk-camping .co.uk, tel.: 01760 441300). An 11-acre site made up with several camping paddocks and surrounded by woodland. 14 miles from The Dower House.

Top: The Dower House campsite
Bottom Left: Caravans at The Dower House
Bottom Right: Thorpe Woodlands

The Orchard Campsite
Suffolk

Orchards. Forbidden fruits. Garden of Eden. Paradise? The Orchard Campsite, tucked into 4 acres of Suffolk countryside, is some way close to paradise and there's not too much that's forbidden either. This is an incredibly family-friendly place, where children are treated like royalty and without a horde of 'Don't …' or 'No …' signs to clutter up the site.

Okay, let's get the downside over with because there's only one: despite its rural, verdant location, with trees galore and all the rest that's good, there can be quite a lot of road noise from the main A12. Located on the outskirts of the very pretty town of Wickham Market, you can't see the dual-carriageway from the campsite, as there's a good high hedge, but there's no denying you can hear it, although it does quieten off at night and if you live on a busy town road you'll think nothing of it.

That said, the site is beautiful. Orchard and woodland run down to the River Deben, where you can drop a line for perch and pike or launch a kayak to paddle all the way to Woodbridge and the coast if your arms hold out. The slightly sloping area called 'The Meadow' is where the six hook-ups are; it's advisable to make sure you've got levellers unless you like the idea of rolling out of bed, and RVs or 'vans over 7 metres might struggle with access. There's still the odd fruit tree for shade and seasonal interest. The secluded woodland and pond areas are kept for tents but all visitors can enjoy the grounds.

A lot of work has been happening in the wood in recent times, with an open coppice next to the river that's full of very tall Cricket Bat willows, so straight you can almost hear the sound of leather against, well, willow. More trees have been planted and the ground has been returfed to allow more campers to be able to stay in the woodland area.

Above: The play area in the site's garden

There's a mummy and a baby pond, with the mummy stopping several koi carp from escaping. The baby pond is full of newts, frog spawn and all sorts of other goodies, suitable for a jam-jar education, that creep, crawl and hide among the rushes and the undergrowth. Little nippers looking to do unthinkable deeds with their new-found scientific specimens can have their attention diverted by pointing out the small

Left: The River Deben, which borders the campsite

play area in the garden and by nightfall, when the campfires are crackling, they'll have forgotten all about their water-born torture subjects.

On busy weekends and holidays, when children outnumber parents, out come the glow sticks. Once a blanket of darkness falls and the stars show their shiny faces, the Glow-stick Scavenge begins: the luminous rods are hurled into space, ready for the ensuing sprint as they fall to earth in some giant game of pick-up sticks. An evening of fun prevails, the children kept amused with the simplest of construction games, assembling glow-in-the-dark creations. It would keep them going all night if the fresh Suffolk air didn't stifle their energy, as the sleep-inducing outdoor ventilation presses heavy on the eyelids.

When the time comes to leave the pond life to look after itself while you head out into the countryside, Wickham Market is a good starting point before moving on to larger towns such as Woodbridge and Ipswich. And it's only a 20-minute drive to the coast – the wetland habitat of the RSPB Nature Reserve at Orford Ness will appeal to bird lovers.

Snape Maltings will provide a day's activities of shopping, eating, river walks and gallery exhibitions, all in a picturesque location by the River Alde. And, of course, there's the Aldeburgh Festival, founded by Suffolk's most celebrated composer, Benjamin Britten, and his friends. There's a farmers' market held each month at Snape Maltings, but to experience life down on the farm, head for Jimmy's Farm (of Jimmy Doherty television fame) at Wherstead just south of Ipswich and another 20-minute drive from the campsite. You can wander about the farm, meet the animals, go on a nature trail or eat outdoors in the Field Kitchen or indoors at Jimmy's Restaurant, housed in a 200-year old timber-framed barn.

The Orchard Campsite

28 Spring Lane, Wickham Market, Suffolk, IP13 0SJ

07818 034729

www.orchardcampsite.co.uk

orchardcampsite@gmail.com

Opening times: Open all year

Facilities: Pitches for 'vans and tents, hook-ups, showers and toilets, shaver points, kitchen with dishwashing, microwave and washing machine, chemical toilet disposal point, small shop with off-licence and bar, barbecue area, play area, campfires and firewood, fishing, canoe launch.

How to get there: From A12 east of Ipswich, take the exit signed Wickham Market. If coming from south, turn right shortly after the town's market place into Spring Lane. If coming from north, take third left into Spring Lane. Site is half a mile on left with tight turn.

Food & drink: The Farm Café & Food Market (www.farmcafe.co.uk, tel.: 01728 747717). Directly on the A12 just north of Wickham Market, great lunches, afternoon teas and a superb farm-shop-style indoor market offering Suffolk-grown produce.

Nearby attractions: Spend a day working in the vines at Shawsgate Vineyard (www.shawsgate.co.uk, tel.: 01728 764060). If that's too much like hard work, you can picnic in the vines and buy a bottle to take home.

Alternative campsite: Tangham Campsite (www.forestcamping.co.uk, tel.: 01394 450707). Campsite in the woods opposite Rendlesham Forest Centre, the forest made famous by an alleged alien landing some years ago!

Top: Lots of space for relaxing at the campsite
Bottom Left: The Orchard Campsite
Bottom Right: Lady's Smock wildflowers at the campsite

Run Cottage
Suffolk

There's something quintessentially English about church bells ringing, and when it happens as you arrive at a campsite, what more of a welcome could you want? Of course you need to arrive on the hour to receive that campanologist's salutation from All Saints' Church, a mere bell-pull away from Run Cottage, but those dulcet tones give an instant 'good-to-be-in-England' feeling.

Above: Run Cottage Touring Park

Not that you need any additional welcome, thanks to the warmth coming from the welcome provided by Michele and Andrew, who own the site and live in Run Cottage. Their gentle demeanour and soothing, unhurried approach will have you chilled out before you've so much as unhitched and levelled up.

Andrew is a true craftsman, a real man of the country. It's just possible that when you arrive, he'll greet you

in his overalls. It's with no disrespect to you, it's just that he's often in the middle of making a weather vane or some decorative wrought-iron plant stand and you've struck while the iron is hot. Some of his blacksmithing work is on display in the campsite information room, where there's also all sorts of interesting facts on walks to local pubs, a book exchange and a library of magazines.

Driving to Run Cottage takes a little while once you come off the main A12. Cutting through woodland and across the open heathland of Hollesley Common, filled with prickly gorse and stunted pines, it feels as if you're heading for the back of beyond. And you pretty much are, for if you were to drive a mile *beyond* the campsite, you would fall into the sea over the shingle sands. You can't actually see the water from the campsite, but wander a couple of hundred yards up the little lane away from the village and you'll catch a glimpse of it, across the pancake-flat, open fields that are all between you and the easterly wind.

The campsite is sheltered from such blasts of cool air. A short way out of the village, it sits well back from the not-very-busy lane and is surrounded by tall trees, yet is far from gloomy or dark, as the birches allow in lots of sunlight; there's also a small coppice for walking pooches behind the site that catches any impending breeze.

Right: Looking across the pond at Run Cottage to the village church

There are 45 pitches, all with hook-ups, that are laid out on grass around the outside of the site and on hardstandings in the middle. Shrubs and small hedges break up the pitches and flowers adorn the site; it's always kept in tip-top condition. Andrew commented that the first thing some visitors do is rush to check out the loos, hoping for something akin to their home comforts. Putting sanitation as top priority above the rest of the site, and all it has to offer, is not considered obligatory for many (especially as most 'vans have all their own facilities), but, for those interested, the toilets and showers are very smart, indeed some of the finest you'll come across.

Run Cottage does tend to attract child-free couples – not that they stipulate 'adults only', but there are no obvious entertainments for children; no playground or games room. But if the little ones enjoy the natural world and are easily entertained with long walks or visiting local attractions, they'll find the peaceful surroundings equally enjoyable as their grown-up counterparts, with the chance to watch out for local wildlife on the pond or in the small stream that drifts down one side of the park; sit still and you might just catch the white streak of the majestic barn owl swooping low at dusk, searching for his supper.

As the leaves, tinged with pink, flutter to the ground and begin to crunch, when others have booked their caravans into storage until spring, aired the soft furnishings and forgotten to leave the fridge door ajar to stop something furry growing, eager winter tourers can have the run of the place. The summer flowers might have gone, the easterly wind might not be so warm, but the frost, clinging to the trees, looks equally enchanting and nature continues to play its part in the world of entertainment. And the bells continue to chime.

Run Cottage Touring Park

Alderton Road, Hollesley, Woodbridge, Suffolk
IP12 3RQ

01394 411309

www.runcottage.co.uk

info@runcottage.co.uk

Opening times: Open all year

Facilities: 45 pitches (14 hardstanding), hook-ups, free hot showers, very clean toilets, chemical toilet disposal point, dog walk, information room, dishwashing and laundry, 2 glamping pods. Dogs welcome.

How to get there: From A12, turn right onto A1152, signed Bawdsey, then B1083, signed Bawdsey and Hollesley. In three-quarters of a mile fork left, signed Hollesley. After 5 miles, on entering Hollesley, turn right into The Street. Site is on the edge of the village, 100 yards past a red-brick bridge.

Food & drink: The Shepherd and Dog (www.shepherdand doghollesley.co.uk, tel.: 01394 411855) in Hollesley and within walking distance of the campsite serves excellent home-cooked pub food. For a pub with a view, the Ramsholt Arms (www.the ramsholtarms.com; tel.: 01394 411209), in the neighbouring village of Ramsholt, has a lovely garden overlooking the River Deben just before it enters the sea.

Nearby attractions: Orford Ness Nature Reserve has the largest vegetated shingle spit in Europe and has a secret military history of Cold War testing. Sutton Hoo is the important burial site of an Anglo-Saxon warrior king; it was uncovered along with helmets, weapons and royal treasure and is set in a 245-acre estate with wildlife walks.

Alternative campsite: Tangham Campsite (www.forestcamping.co.uk, tel.: 01394 450707). Camping among the trees at Rendlesham Forest Centre, 4 miles from Run Cottage.

Top Left: The pond at Run Cottage
Top Right: Pitches at Run Cottage Touring Park
Bottom: Shrubs and small hedges offer privacy to individual pitches

Waterclose Meadows
Cambridgeshire

As agricultural architecture goes, Houghton Mill (pronounced **Ho-ton**) is as pleasing to the eye as any; the soft-brick and black-weatherboarded structure straddles the glistening Great Ouse like an elderly guardian. Indeed, the 18th-century building is the only watermill on the river that still works, with wheat still being ground in the traditional way using water-powered millstones. You can watch flour being made and, if you fancy making a loaf, buy the end product. Even when the cogs, wheels and pulleys are not in action, you can still wander around the mill and marvel at the simplicity of the technology, imagining life in a bygone era, when the air was thick with dust. Now a tranquil calm resides in the air, the lungs able to draw in large gulps of a fresh, riverside atmosphere.

Waterclose Meadows Campsite sits in the adjoining meadow, with superb views of the nearby mill, behind which the sun sets creating beautiful silhouettes. There are good views of the mill pond, too, created from a backwater of the Great Ouse, and the pointing finger of the church spire in the village of Houghton.

The campsite at Houghton Mill is a cosy, all-grass site with gravel tracks and surrounded by high hedges; the 54 pitches are broken up by wild cherry and birch trees. And with no roads passing the site and relatively poor mobile-phone reception, it's a place where more twittering comes from the hedgerows than the laptop, where hand-held blackberries stain your fingers and

texting is a read through the Sunday papers; this is, in all, a quiet site. There's no playground, no entertainment laid on. It's one for lovers of the great outdoors who like to make their own fun, where nature walks along the river, identifying dragonflies and spotting fish before the heron does, are the activities for the day.

Above: Under the cherry trees at the campsite

It's a mostly level site, although ramps and levellers will help to smooth out the odd ripple in the ground, and every pitch has electric hook-ups. Standards of maintenance are high, with the site always looking immaculate.

The National Trust owns and manages the land around Houghton Mill, including the mill and the campsite itself. There are plenty of waymarked paths along the river and across the flood meadows that can be accessed direct from the campsite, with abundant wildlife, river views and distant church spires to survey. It's a popular stroll for dog-walkers too. Much of the fishing is restricted to members of a local angling club, but there's free fishing on the backwater directly in front of the campsite (i.e. on the mill pond) and accessible club-managed fishing on the Great Ouse, behind the mill at Hemingford Meadows; day tickets can be purchased at the tackle shop in the village.

The village of Houghton, a few paces from the mill, is a 'traditional' Huntingdonshire hamlet with winding lanes and timber-framed houses so crooked they'd give many a structural engineer incontrollable spasms even though, centuries on, they're still standing. At the village centre stands a rare thatched clock tower, providing a gentle nudge in the ribs for anyone who has propped up a table outside the neighbouring Three Horseshoes for too long in the midday sun.

Following the Great Ouse east, the small town of St Ives is within walking distance (1¾ miles) of the campsite and sits on the river. Stand on the old stone bridge, upon which is a miniscule chapel, for views back across the water meadows to Houghton. Alternatively, make the most of the waterway with a trip upstream, spotting wildlife from the water, with St Ives Electric Riverboat Co. Scheduled trips start from The Quay, in the town centre, at weekends from May to September. The ancient town has lots of places to eat, some on the water's edge, others lining Market Hill, the wide boulevard that houses regular markets.

Elsewhere in the area, the landscape is criss-crossed with rivers and fens, the most famous Wicken Fen, a National Trust nature reserve and an important wetland area; there you can view rare species of wildlife, such as hen harriers, and cross reedbeds on raised boardwalks.

Waterclose Meadows Campsite

Houghton Mill, Mill Street, Houghton, Huntingdon, PE28 2AZ

01480 466716

www.nationaltrust.org.uk/houghton-mill

houghtonmillcampsite@nationaltrust.org.uk

Opening times: March to October

Facilities: 54 pitches, all with hook-ups; amenity block with free showers, toilets, washbasins, laundry room, vegetable preparation area, reception area selling gas and information on the local area. Amenity block immaculate. Dogs welcome.

How to get there: A1123 St Ives/Huntingdon road. Turn off signposted Houghton/Houghton Mill. In village, cross the market square into Mill Street, pass church on right, turn left immediately before last house – a tight turning. No arrivals before 1 pm or after 8 pm.

Food & drink: The Three Horseshoes (www.threehorseshoes innhoughton.co.uk, tel.: 01480 462410) in Houghton serves real ales and a varied menu from pub classics to seasonal fare and is within walking distance of the campsite. Cream teas are served at the National Trust tea room next to the mill. For a gastro-pub with a great reputation for food, try The White Hart (www.whitehart-godmanchester.co.uk, tel.: 01480 414050) in nearby Godmanchester.

Nearby attractions: The National Trust-owned Houghton Mill, plus Wicken Fen, Wimpole Hall and Farm. St Ives and the city of Cambridge are both a short drive from the campsite.

Alternative campsite: Wyton Lakes Holiday Park (www.wytonlakes.com, tel.: 01480 412715). An adults-only site on the A1123, a mile from Waterclose Meadows.

Top: The pretty village of Houghton
Bottom Left: The campsite grounds
Bottom Right: Scenic riverside walks from the campsite

Lincoln Farm Park
Oxfordshire

Neither near Lincoln or associated any longer with a farm, Lincoln Farm Park is a puzzling name for this touring park. Unlike many of the sites in this book, Lincoln Farm Park is right in the centre of a village, Standlake, and a very pretty village too, with well-proportioned, sandy-coloured houses that fit the character of the county. The minnow-sized River Windrush ebbs its way through the village to join up with its mightier partner, the River Thames, 2 miles south, where water meadows flatten out the land and fishermen cast a line for an 'it was this big' catch.

Above: Christ Church College, one of many tourist attractions in Oxford

Lincoln Farm Park stamps its mark over 8 acres of village territory, which sounds vast. However, this is no windswept open field; the site snuggles in among the houses and then screens itself with a whole hedge of ever-maturing trees so as not to irritate the neighbours

or for them to annoy you. The site is then split up into neat little areas using post-and-rail fences, laurel and beech hedges and willows that weep to the ground, interspersed with a smattering of wild cherry trees and shrubs. The gardeners are regularly on the scene, tidying up or planting, and they're a cheery bunch of fellows. All the pitches are level and hardstanding, with manicured lawns between for throwing out a picnic rug. The park has won a cabinet full of awards, with certificates papering the wall by reception, where yet more cheery staff welcome you with friendly banter and a smile. Its facilities have been granted five-star status and it is one of a group of prestigious, privately owned, top-notch sites known as the 'Best of British'.

In fact, the site is so manicured and pristine that you start to look for a certain something that will lift it from the crowd of perfect but oh-so-dull (because they all look the same and offer the same facilities) touring parks. It's certainly got that something.

There is not one but two indoor swimming pools that wouldn't look out of place in a luxury health spa. And for the shyest of bikini-revealing folk, or for those who merely prefer not to be dive-bombed by a posse of marauding teenagers, you can book both pools for private hire for less coinage than a family trip to the local pool with added milkshakes. Thrown into the price is the private use of the full shebang – connected to each pool is a sauna, a bubbling spa pool and, in

Right: The River Thames south of Standlake

'Pool Two', a steam room and small children's pool where you can keep an eye on little splashers from the depths of your own supersize bath. Comfy seating is supplied too. Both pools are stunningly immaculate and in quite superb surroundings with pine-clad ceilings and mosaic-tiled surrounds. The pools are worthy of a stay at the park just for the whole private-hire experience, but should your enthusiasm for the water deflate as quickly as a cheap lilo, there's plenty else on offer in the county.

With the Thames a couple of miles away, so is the accompanying Thames Path, which follows the river from its source in neighbouring Gloucestershire through the upper reaches of the quieter and more immature river, where its soulmates are often little more than a dazzling kingfisher and a field full of daisies. By the time the Thames reaches the dizzying spires of Oxford, 10 miles from the campsite by road or 14 miles by river, it has changed name, temporarily, as the locals fondly refer to it as the Isis for reasons better known to the city's Inspector Morse (something to do with which river is the tributary of which). Port Meadow is a grand picnic spot and a great introduction to Oxford if arriving by river. In the city centre, boaters can swap motor power for muscle power and take an idyllic punt on the River Cherwell, Oxford's notable other.

In general, Oxford is awash with ornate architecture and enough bicycles to rival Beijing. You can add your bike to the cycle racks and take a guided tour of the colleges on foot. Climb the Carfax Tower for an eye tour of the city's spires and rooftops before heading to the famous Covered Market to sample one of the quirky student cafes, where a large latte and a good book can last all morning.

Then back to the campsite to dive into that private pool again. What a life …

Lincoln Farm Park

High Street, Standlake, Witney, Oxfordshire, OX29 7RH

01865 300239

www.lincolnfarmpark.co.uk

info@lincolnfarmpark.co.uk

Opening times: Beginning of February to mid-November

Facilities: 90 pitches, all with hook-ups, free showers in heated amenity building, baby-changing rooms and family bathroom, disabled facilities, laundry, dishwashing, large shop with gas sales, play area, dog walk, indoor leisure centre with swimming pools plus fitness centre. Dogs welcome.

How to get there: A415 from Abingdon to Witney. Entering Standlake, turn into the High Street by the village garage. The site is 300 metres farther on the right.

Food & drink: There are two good pubs in the village, but for a spot of magic, go to The Trout Inn (www.thetroutoxford.co.uk, tel.: 01865 510930) at Wolvercote. Overlooking the Thames, it has one of the finest locations in the county.

Nearby attractions: The campsite has a well-placed central location in the country on the fringes of the Cotswolds. Oxford can be accessed by bus from the stop just outside the campsite. Blenheim Palace is 10 miles away.

Alternative campsite: Hardwick Park (www.hardwickparks.co.uk, tel.: 01865 300501). A large touring site (with holiday homes) by the River Windrush and a series of lakes with watersports facilities.

Top: One of two pools to hire privately
Bottom Left: The countryside around Standlake
Bottom Right: Lincoln Farm Park

Hurley Riverside Park
Berkshire

Believe me, my young friend, there is nothing – absolutely nothing – half so much worth doing as simply messing about in boats.

The Wind in the Willows, *Kenneth Grahame*

Above: A camper van at Hurley Riverside Park

If you haven't got a boat, the next best thing must be messing about by the river. And you can just imagine Ratty and Mole beside the River Thames at Hurley with their tablecloth laid out on the riverbank, luncheon basket open, tucking into the cold chicken. There are people messing about in boats, too, ambling through the water, dodging the overhanging willow branches, and generally having a good time. Hurley is an incredibly picturesque riverside village between Henley-on-Thames and Marlow. For many it's commuter territory – grand houses with large gardens and private moorings – for others it's a playground. Here, the river

is potentially at its busiest, bar the stretch between Putney and Tower Bridge.

The name's a dead giveaway, but it's here that Hurley Riverside Park has set up camp. The main site is a few boat lengths away from the Norman village, but it's connected by the Riverside Picnic Grounds, a kilometre of riverbank space that's owned by the park and for use by its visitors.

The touring area is a large site that has been carefully broken up into ten paddocks of varying size, screened and enclosed by tall hedges and trees filled with birdsong. Most of the pitches are placed round the edges of each paddock but, owing to their irregular shapes, it doesn't feel as if you've been parked on sentry duty. Most pitches are on grass (there's a very limited number of hardstandings), giving the site a very rural feel. Plenty of water points are located in convenient positions for each paddock, and three timber-lodge style amenity blocks blend in as well as they can. The site is well away from the road, down a long drive, so it's very peaceful, with the exception of the odd Heathrow-bound flight overhead. There are some static holiday homes that are kept entirely separate, away from the touring area.

There are few immediate views – you cannot actually see the river from the touring pitches because of the thick hedges and ancient oaks around the site

boundary – but one attraction is very noticeable: a large white castellated building that dominates the skyline, cut among the hillside woodland. Once a luxurious officers' mess, this early 19th-century pile is now the upmarket Danesfield House Hotel, with amazing formal Italianate gardens and an afternoon tea worthy of a visit, plus an oak-panelled dining room with award-winning food if you're celebrating something extra special and the caravan stove doesn't quite pass muster.

The Thames is only feet away from the campsite and there is direct access to a water meadow for cartwheeling through or whatever takes your fancy. Casting a line is allowed, subject to all the usual national rules; the park has its own water bailiff who comes round and charges a nominal fee for the day. Those who want to follow Ratty's dream and drop a small boat or a canoe in the water can do so via the slipway in the Picnic Grounds. Hurley Lock and Weir is renowned as one of the best places for freestyle kayaking because of the waves created when the lock gates are open, attracting white-water thrill-seekers from around the world.

Those preferring dry land can still appreciate the joys of the river by meandering along the Thames Path, which runs past the campsite. You can either catch the morning sun by strolling towards Bisham Abbey, now a major National Sports Centre, and onto the quaint riverside town of Marlow, or watch the sun set by aimlessly dawdling towards Henley-on-Thames. There you can hire a boat from Hobbs of Henley to mess about on the river or pay a visit to the River and Rowing Museum, where Kenneth Grahame's Ratty, Mole and Toad come to life in their own permanent exhibition. And if you don't manage to see them there, when you're back at the campsite sit very still – you never know who might come rowing down the river.

Hurley Riverside Park

Hurley, Berkshire, SL6 5NE

01628 824493

www.hurleyriversidepark.co.uk

info@hurleyriversidepark.co.uk

Opening times: Beginning of March to end of October

Facilities: 208 pitches (37 hardstanding), electric hook-ups, hot showers, family showers, disabled facilities, laundry room, dishwashing area, chemical toilet disposal points, playground, on-site shop, picnic grounds with slipway. Dogs welcome.

How to get there: Junction 8/9 of M4 or junction 4 of M40. A404. A4130, signed Henley-on-Thames. Ignore signs for Hurley village. The driveway for the campsite is on the right, half a mile past the turning for Hurley village.

Food & drink: Ye Olde Bell Inn, Hurley (www.theoldebell.co.uk, tel.: 01628 825881). Top-notch ancient pub with ambience and fine food served indoors and out.

Nearby attractions: Windsor and the time-warped village of Eton are 15 miles from the site, Legoland is a similar distance. There are several National Trust properties within a 10-mile radius.

Alternative campsite: Swiss Farm International (www.swissfarmcamping.co.uk, tel.: 01491 573419). Large site on the outskirts of Henley-on-Thames, 5 miles from Hurley.

Left: Hurley Riverside Park
Top Right: The village of Hurley
Bottom Right: Blossoms in spring on the site

Wellington Country Park
Berkshire

You know that something's different about the campsite at Wellington Country Park as soon as you're handed a map of the site. It's shaped like a giant tree, the leaves and branches creating small enclosures so each 'van is with no more than another three campers. Wandering around the site, there's no telling that it's marked out like an old oak but the small, intimate clusters of 'vans is noticeable, as are the spacious and private pitches.

The aptness of the tree-shaped site is not lost either – this is a woodland site after all, where 'vans disappear among the oaks, birches, pines and hollies. The woodland floor is laid with wild flowers and bracken. While it's pleasantly dense enough to feel cosy, light still filters through the treetops to signal a dawn chorus from chirpy birds. At night, however comforting the duvet might feel, peek through the door to see real darkness and to listen to the silence; there are no lights on the campsite so, in a country so often filled with the glow of sodium orange and luminous pollution, finding the truth about the dark can be an enlightening experience. And don't forget a torch in case you want a late-night wander.

All the caravan and motorhome pitches are hard-standing; after a fresh shower the woodland floor gives off sweet smells, but the ground can get quite soggy under the trees.

If there's a downside, it's not being able to arrive after 5.30 pm, or 4.30 pm in low season, when the reception area shuts and the campsite is locked up behind a slightly disconcerting but securely padlocked gate, the key for which is obtained from reception. However, the upside is free use of Wellington Country Park, a 350-acre parkland estate that engulfs the campsite.

Above: Anemones carpet the floor

Wellington Country Park provides a total change of scenery from the residential woodland; as you wander through the park entrance, you may experience shock mingled with a stirring of the soul – an open-plan vista with an enormous lake, large enough to sink a small village, greets you. The lake is filled with ducks, geese, grebes and various other aquatic fowl that call the one-time gravel pit home. What's refreshing to see, in a large country park that's open to the paying public, is that the lake has been left to nature; the swans and their chums are master and don't have to fight with a series of boats plying the water. The green meadows around the edge are a great place for a picnic, providing the ducks don't pinch your sandwiches, and barbecues are allowed. Elsewhere in the park, hidden among the trees, are lots of playground activities for children. Again, it's free to all campsite residents and you can take it or leave it according to your preference for man-made entertainment or pure nature. Be warned: you'll have a hard task prising the children away should they catch glimpse of the Play Trail or the Enchanted Forest.

If nature is more your plan for the day, the park has devised four walking trails varying in length and focusing on different aspects: woodland, waterfowl, birdwatching and antler spotting. The antlers refer to the red and fallow deer that reside in the area adjacent to the campsite; the deer blend in well to the woodland glade, their impressive branch-like antlers bringing tears to the eyes both for their beauty and at the prospect of being on the receiving end of one.

The deer's home, Waterloo Meadow, refers neither to any aqueous pasture nor to Abba's Eurovision winner, but to the historic battle that put the park owner's ancestor firmly in the public eye. The country park is owned by the ninth Duke of Wellington. His parents established the park in the seventies (when the growing Thames population was becoming increasingly urban) in the hope that it would provide a place for the public to enjoy and develop a love of the countryside.

If you fancy a little look at the duke's des-res, Stratfield Saye, it's just 2 miles away next to the River Loddon. The first duke acquired the house in 1817 after his victory over Napoleon and it has been the ancestral home ever since. It might be a little grander than a caravan in the woods, but in our opinion there's nothing to beat that back-to-nature outdoorsy feeling.

Wellington Country Park

Odiham Road, Riseley, Reading, Berkshire, RG7 1SP

0118 932 6444

www.wellington-country-park.co.uk

camping@wellington-country-park.co.uk

Opening times: End of February to beginning of November

Facilities: 87 pitches (51 for caravans), hook-ups (to all caravan pitches), free hot showers, toilets, shaver points, dishwashing, laundry and iron, chemical toilet disposal point, wi-fi available, free access to country park with new play facilities. Dogs welcome.

How to get there: From Junction 11 off M4, A33 towards Basingstoke. After 3 miles, at second roundabout, turn left, signed Wellington Country Park. Site is off the B3349. Alternatively, from Junction 5 off M3, B3349 towards Riseley and Reading, site is on right after 8 miles.

Food & drink: Wellington Farm Shop (www.wellingtonfarmshop .co.uk, tel.: 0118 932 6132). The estate's farm shop sells its own Hereford beef, plus lamb and game reared on the estate. There's honey from the estate's hives, plus lots of other meats, deli products, seasonal UK-grown fruit and veg and essential items from local sources.

Nearby attractions: Stratfield Saye House (www.wellington estates.co.uk), home of the Duke of Wellington, is open to the public. In the grounds is the grave of Copenhagen, the horse that helped the first Duke of Wellington to victory at Waterloo. There's an exhibition on the first Duke too.

Alternative campsite: California Chalet & Touring Park (www.californiaholidaypark.com, tel.: 0844 682 0357). Another site in a woodland setting five crow-miles but 12 road-miles from Wellington Country Park.

Top Left: Swans live on the lake
Bottom Left: Private pitches at the campsite
Right: Woodland surrounds the campsite

Chertsey
Surrey

Camping doesn't have to mean sitting in a field; sometimes the bright lights beckon and the need to paint the town red or soak up some culture – an evening at the theatre, a visit to a gallery or a museum – comes calling. And there can be nothing better after a hard day's sightseeing than to leave the bustle of the foot-tramping commuters behind and head for the leafy suburbs, particularly when that sightseeing has been in the capital.

There are several campsites situated within the M25, a prospect that seems about as anomalous as a town house in the country. But location's the key and one site really stands out in that respect, the Chertsey Camping & Caravanning Club Site. Open to non-members, it's within a couple of miles of the M25, so reaching it is easy when towing a caravan or driving a large motorhome, but it's not within the capital's Low Emission Zone, an important factor considering the expense that's incurred if you enter the zone with a liable 'van.

The real bonus is the site's riverside setting – there is direct access from the campsite to the banks of the Thames – although something to consider if you're travelling with adventurous, wandering toddlers.

The Thames Path runs past the site too, if stretching the legs down Oxford Street doesn't appeal. Otherwise, access to the West End is a 30-minute

train ride to Waterloo from Weybridge station, 1 mile from the site; bicycles are carried free on the train. Alternatively, a bus from outside the site to Heathrow will connect with regular services on the London Underground (Piccadilly line) direct into the city and the museums at South Kensington, strolls around the Serpentine, concerts on the South Bank, shopping on Bond Street or dim sum in Chinatown. Whatever your preference, just remember, your 'van is waiting for you back at base.

Above: Canoeing from the campsite is possible

There's no getting away from the fact that there is some noise on site – that's the price you pay for urban camping and being within striking distance of London. The hum of road noise is inevitable and, as the site is relatively close to Heathrow, there's also the occasional roar of a jet engine overhead.

Left: The River Thames at Chertsey

But there's plenty of birdsong too, thanks to the numerous mature trees around keeping the site leafy and cool in summer.

The Chertsey site has received a David Bellamy Gold Conservation Award (the enthusiastic chap puts his name to this annual award scheme for campsites) for its wildlife-friendly environment; there's no shortage of little creatures, be it scampering squirrels racing up tree trunks or nesting swans cohabiting with local ducks. A boardwalk and picnic area have been erected overlooking the river and make the perfect place to while away a summer's afternoon, and there are a couple of riverside benches to contemplate the world while becoming transfixed by the river's flow. Anglers can cast a line, too, and canoe launching is possible – the site regularly hosts events by the Canoe-Camping Club.

All the usual facilities that are expected from club sites are available, with immaculately kept showers and loos (the site has been awarded five stars by the national 'Loo of the Year Award'!), laundry facilities and a dog walk, although the Thames Path is more exhilarating. There's wi-fi access for those who need to be logged on. The site is open all year and with plenty of hardstanding pitches so visitors can make the most of city breaks out of season, enjoying the capital's Christmas and New Year festivities. During the drier months, the grass pitches overlooking the elegant Chertsey Bridge are open and you'd be forgiven for forgetting that you were camping in a field again after all.

Chertsey Camping & Caravanning Club Site

Bridge Road, Chertsey, Surrey, KT16 8JX

01932 562405

www.campingandcaravanningclub.co.uk

Opening times: Open all year

Facilities: 150 pitches (65 hardstanding), hook-ups, hot showers, toilets, shaver points, disabled facilities, parent/baby room, laundry, dishwashing, chemical toilet disposal point, motorhome service point, playground, wi-fi, gas exchange, dog walk, fishing, canoe launch point. Dogs welcome.

How to get there: Junction 11 of M25, A317 towards Chertsey, fork right before entering town centre for B375, signed Walton-on-Thames. At traffic lights, turn right onto B375. Site entrance is quarter of a mile farther on the left, before the bridge.

Food & drink: The Crown Hotel, London Street, Chertsey (www.crownchertsey.co.uk, tel.: 01932 564657). A beautiful old coaching inn with great food and a warm atmosphere.

Nearby attractions: There are three racecourses nearby at Epsom, Kempton Park and Sandown Park. For teenagers, Thorpe Park has lots of exhilarating rides and is a couple of miles from the site. Kew Gardens, rugby at Twickenham, golf at Wentworth, plus events at Earls Court and Olympia are all possible from the Chertsey site. For something a bit different, take a walking tour with London Walks (www.londonwalks.com, tel.: 020 7624 3978) – these are guided walks on selected themes using real people (often actors) rather than umbrella-holders to explain a thing or two about the city.

Alternative campsite: Horsley Camping and Caravanning Club Site (www.campingandcaravanningclub.co.uk, tel.: 01483 283273). Just outside the M25, near East Horsley but still within close proximity to a Waterloo-bound train.

Top Left: A campsite pitch at Chertsey
Top Right: Birds frequently nest by the campsite
Bottom: Chertsey Bridge

Tanner Farm Park
Kent

Some campsites have that comfortable feeling the moment you turn into the drive; everything seems to fit into place – the buildings look good, the landscape is well maintained and there's an atmosphere of welcoming serenity. Tanner Farm Park is one such site. Its location helps – the long access lane, off a quiet country road, takes you to nowhere but the park, which sits in the middle of arable farmland and forms part of the Kent Weald.

Above: Tanner Farm Park

The approach is pretty unique for a campsite, past the soft-coloured brick 'oh-so traditional' farmhouse and, on the left, the duck pond and the five-kiln oast houses with each kiln roof pointing skywards like an upturned funnel, a legacy from bygone days when previous generations brought hops from the Kentish fields to the farm for drying.

Through the park's gates, the reception and shop sit in a beautifully restored ancient barn. Then the park opens out, with views across open farmland, and from virtually every pitch you gain sight of the oast house. While many pitches are on hardstanding to cater for all-year-round campers, a large grass area is opened up for the summer months, with places to picnic under the trees and space for little ones to play.

Pet owners can enjoy the walks provided around the farm; visitors have the privilege of walking through the fields and woodland (the North Wood provides a stunning display of bluebells in early summer) that surround the site. And there's plenty of wildlife to enjoy; the chances of opening your curtains in the morning to find a rabbit just outside your 'van are fair. A series of leaflets outlining different circular walks from the campsite, and in many cases passing a watering hole, provide the perfect opportunity to explore the Kentish countryside in detail.

Slightly farther afield, though still within walking or pedalling distance, is Kalmora Spa; here you can pass the time stretched out on a massage couch receiving any number of relaxing or invigorating treatments, or resting in a Dead Sea floatation pool.

When the urge to get a little more energetic arrives, Bedgebury National Pinetum is a good place to head for. Six miles from the campsite, this is the most

Right: Bluebells in North Wood

complete collection of conifers in the world, with
350 acres of trees, including rare and endangered
species. The adjacent 2,000-acre forest has miles of
paths for runners or walkers and specifically designed
orienteering trails, plus many opportunities for cycling
and mountain biking (bike-hire is on site). There's
wheelchair access to parts of the forest, too. An
adventurous playground keeps young children amused
and for daredevil monkeys (minimum age ten years)
there's the chance to swing through the trees on a Go
Ape! high-wire forest adventure course.

Elsewhere in the area, vineyards abound offering tours,
wine shops and bistros. Lamberhurst Vineyard is just
down the road from the campsite, while the Chapel
Down Winery is close by at Tenterden. Organic wine
is made at Sedlescombe Vineyard, with some of their
vines touching the edges of the impressive Bodiam
Castle, just over the county border in East Sussex.

If salty water is more your thing, the south coast
is within easy reach for a day trip – Camber Sands
and the beaches at Hastings are bucket-and-spade
territory. And Bewl Water, the largest inland water in
the south-east, with a perimeter of 17 miles, provides
rowing, canoeing, sailing or a simple pleasure cruise – a
worthwhile way of taking in a different view of the High
Weald Area of Outstanding Natural Beauty.

There's no shortage of beautiful historical places to
visit either – Scotney Castle, Sissinghurst, Bodiam
Castle, Great Dixter, Finchcocks and the 1066 site at
Battle are all within 10 miles of the campsite.

Back at the park, visitors can meet the residents of
the Gold-winning David Bellamy Conservation Award
campsite – it might be the foxes, badgers or weasels
that befriend the woods, the bats flying at dusk or the
numerous birds that also call Tanner Farm Park home.

Tanner Farm Park

Goudhurst Road, Marden, Kent, TN12 9ND

01622 832399

www.tannerfarmpark.co.uk

enquiries@tannerfarmpark.co.uk

Opening times: Open all year

Facilities: 100 pitches, hook-ups, centrally heated shower and toilet blocks, disabled facilities, dishwashing, laundry, chemical toilet disposal point, gas exchange, large shop, playground, dog walk. Dogs welcome.

How to get there: Junction 7 off M25, A229 through Maidstone, signed Staplehurst. Turn right onto B2079, signed Marden. Site is 2 miles past Marden towards Goudhurst on the right.

Food & drink: The Star & Eagle (tel.: 01580 211512) next to the church in Goudhurst. A lovely building, great food and superb views across the Weald.

Nearby attractions: Open all year, Kew at Wakehurst Place (www.kew.org) holds the Millennium Seed Bank run by the Royal Botanical Gardens. There's lots to see in the conservation areas, nature reserves, woodlands and formal botanic gardens, with events throughout the year. The moated Leeds Castle is approximately 8 miles from the campsite, with 500 acres of parkland to wander through. Royal Tunbridge Wells is a 20-minute drive from the campsite too.

Alternative campsite: Still Acres Touring & Camping Park (www.stillacres.com, tel.: 01892 732135) is an adults-only campsite also in Marden and five minutes from Tanner Farm Park.

Left: Lots of open space at Tanner Farm Park
Top Right: Bluebells at the campsite
Bottom Right: The Oast House points to the sky

Denny Wood
Hampshire

Once upon a time a chap named Guillaume lived in France and was quite good at winning fights and conquering land. Sure of his rights to own a piece of England through some highly dodgy claims to blood relatives and a spot of bartering made with the one-time exiled English king, Edward the Confessor – the throne in exchange for a safe house – he nipped across the Channel, won another, quite big, battle and claimed the kingdom. England was never the same again, and during his reign, William the Conqueror stumbled across some deer-filled woods and heathland on the south coast and decided it would make an excellent playground for the exclusive use of his hunting chums.

The best part of a thousand years later, the New Forest is now a playground for all, where commoners have the rights to graze ponies and cattle and visitors can play among the ancient forests. It's a great place for those with motorhomes and caravans, too, with easy-to-drive roads and lots of places to park without the dreaded height barrier. Wild camping is forbidden, but there really is no need with so many excellent campsites.

It's almost criminal to have to choose just one of the Camping in the Forest campsites in the New Forest for this book; realistically, they're all suitable for inclusion. They represent what camping is all about – freedom, space, back to nature and a love of the great outdoors.

Each of the sites attracts different kinds of campers and has its own characteristics according to which part of the New Forest it is based in and what else is around. Of all of them, I've plumped for Denny Wood, which is neither too big nor too small and feels just right. It's one of the quieter sites, being well away from the road, so birdsong and the vibrating shake of the woodpecker are not intruded upon. There's also a mix of open, grassy glade and parkland-style woodland

Above: New Forest ponies frequent the campsite

with oak, beech and chestnuts still allowing plenty of dappled light to filter through. With no toilet or shower facilities on site, it's truly back to basics (there are waste disposal and water points) and, refreshingly void of hook-ups, you can pitch where you like depending on whether you wish to catch the full sun or keep under the shade; simple common sense dictates that

Left: A pony grazing near a motorhome at Denny Wood

you don't pitch so close to your neighbours to create a fire hazard – but then, who doesn't want a bit of space? That's what you've come for.

The very likeable ponies saunter through from time to time, seemingly oblivious to onlookers and their 'vans. You really can get very close to them, although touching is not recommended; on the whole they're very docile but something might just spook them.

Open campfires are, hardly surprisingly, not allowed, although sizzling a sausage on a barbecue is okay so long as it's raised off the ground. When the smoke has drifted into the trees and the washing up is done, why not follow the woodland smells, trundle through the bracken on the forest floor, listen for the cuckoo and watch the woodpecker dip and dive from trunk to trunk. The trees are well spaced, so it's not an imposing woodland; there's plenty of space in the grassy glades around the site for kicking a ball or sliding down the base of a tree with a half-read novel and eyelids that feel like treacle.

Denny Wood is one of the best placed of the Camping in the Forest sites, too. It is located well within the National Park and sits close to a B-road that's easy to drive and which accesses Beaulieu, home to the National Motor Museum, where a 1926 Eccles Company caravan is on display. Quite a stunner she is too!

Lyndhurst, the 'capital' of the National Park, is only 3 miles away, with the New Forest Centre providing historical information about the forest. You can get sporty and hire kayaks or canoes to float down the Beaulieu River, but there's just as much strenuous activity to be had cycling from the Denny Wood campsite to the lovely village of Brockenhurst. You can do this without venturing onto any roads, a cycle trail taking you all the way.

Denny Wood Campsite

Beaulieu Road, Lyndhurst, Hampshire, SO43 7FZ

02380 293144

www.campingintheforest.co.uk

Opening times: End of March to end of September

Facilities: 170 pitches, chemical toilet disposal point, water points. No dogs allowed at Denny Wood.

How to get there: Junction 1 on M27. A397 to Lyndhurst. B3056 towards Beaulieu. Site is 2 miles from Lyndhurst on the right.

Food & drink: Pondhead Farm Shop (tel.: 02380 282003) is on the same road, half a mile from Denny Wood towards Lyndhurst, and sells beef, pork and venison from animals raised around the farm and heathland. The New Forest marque on food will guarantee it's local.

Nearby attractions: Head to Hythe for a pretty seafront and boat trips. Buckler's Hard is a lovely village to stop off at.

Alternative campsite: Any of the other Camping in the Forest sites (www.campingintheforest.co.uk) within the New Forest. In particular, **Matley Wood** (tel.: 02380 293144) is the closest to Denny Wood, a matter of a few yards away, and **Setthorns** (tel.: 01590 681020), in denser woodland, is the quietest of the sites and is open all year.

Left: The open glades at Denny Wood
Top Right: A resting pony at the campsite
Bottom Right: Denny Wood is filled with ancient oak, beech and chestnut trees

Chine Farm
Isle of Wight

Diamonds are forever and this particular little diamond of land has indeed been around forever – well, since the dinosaurs at least. Erosion may well have shaped this precious stone over time, cutting back the rocks to reveal the gems that lie beneath – fossils – and the south-western beaches of the diamond-shaped Isle of Wight have some of the best fossil-hunting in Europe.

Above: A Small Copper butterfly feeding from the sea-thrift

As well as dinosaurs, royalty has graced the island's shores with varying degrees of success. The exiled Charles I, looking for a home, hoped for tea and sympathy from the island, only to be imprisoned at Carisbrooke Castle before facing the executioner in 1649. By Victorian times royalty was faring a little better, and the Queen and Prince Albert made Osborne House their summer bolt-hole, making the island seasonally fashionable.

The island now welcomes all sorts of visitors with gracious arms, hosting a range of events, from the Isle of Wight Festival for music lovers to Cowes Week for sailing fans, and it continues to enjoy an influx of seasonal migration in search of the warmer seas and sunnier days from which the island benefits.

The island feels like a mini-Britain, having all the diverse features (except a mountain) of the British Isles in one small space: tall hills and downs, heathland, rolling agricultural countryside, white cliffs, pink cliffs (the residues of a desert existence for our dinosaurs), sandy and shingle beaches, river estuaries, traditional seaside towns, country parks, wetland areas, forests and woodlands – the list goes on.

More than half of the island, mainly the western half, is designated an Area of Outstanding Natural Beauty. It's in this area, perched above the dinosaur bones, that Chine Farm Camping Site sits. To all intents and purposes the site is four flat fields separated by some hedges for shelter when the wind blows (and it can blow hard) and bordered on one side by a reasonably quiet coastal road. Fortunately, it's not the road you hear but the sea, as it laps into Brighstone Bay, particularly if you're on the farthest reaches of the campsite as far as you dare to park against the pink cliff edge. Precariously perched, it's a spectacular spot for a pitch but there are no guards or fences and the bordering Cowleaze Chine (a chine is a steep-sided valley where the river flows

Right: The pink cliff edge at Chine Farm Camping Site

through coastal cliffs to the sea) is steep too, so young families may prefer the safer option of the rear fields which also house a small playground.

From the top of the cliff, visitors are spoilt for a choice of views: there the downs that rise above the coast or the sweeping curve of Brighstone Bay and Compton Bay round towards the far western tip of the island where the cliffs turn chalky white. Below the campsite is the part sand, part shingle beach with access via a footpath. It sadly collects a fair amount of rubbish, though that's not the fault of the campsite, which is kept beautifully clean. Hook-ups are in the most sheltered field only, but consequently with lesser views of the cliffs. It's best, if you can, to go without electrics and pick a prime spot closer to the beach.

Jill and Jeffrey run the site and their small farm from the house across the road. They're cheerful folk who take pride in keeping the site well maintained and will guarantee visitors booked in advance lots of space. If you turn up unannounced in high season, they'll do their best to accommodate you, but you'll have to take pot luck as to where they can place you, although there's almost always a good view. Particularly when there's pin-cushion clumps of pink sea thrift that draw your eye to the cliff top, or the azure blue waters of Compton Bay, a surfer's hot spot. The sea fishing is good, too, and the walks – it's no wonder the island holds an annual month-long walking festival – with the Isle of Wight Coast Path running right past the campsite.

If you decide that your motorhome is simply too big for touring a small island and you fancy something a bit retro, why not leave your beast at home and tour in an old VW camper van from Isle of Wight Campers (www.isleofwightcampers.co.uk, tel.: 01983 642143)? Everything's supplied – including a hamper of local eats – all you have to do is turn up on the ferry.

Chine Farm Camping Site

Military Road, Atherfield Bay, Ventnor,
Isle of Wight, PO38 2JH

01983 740901

www.chine-farm.co.uk

jill@chine-farm.co.uk

Opening times: Easter to end of September

Facilities: 80 pitches, 19 hook-ups, clean amenity building with toilets and free hot showers, dishwashing area, laundry service, chemical toilet disposal point, camping gas exchange, small playground. Dogs welcome.

How to get there: Red Funnel Ferries (www.redfunnel.co.uk, tel.: 0844 844 9988) from Southampton to East Cowes. A3021 to Newport. B3323 to Shorwell. B3399 to Chale. Turn right onto A3055, site is 2 miles farther on the left with reception on the right.

Food & drink: The Garlic Farm Restaurant and Allium Cafe (www.thegarlicfarm.co.uk, tel: 01983 86733) offers a tasty and nutritious menu; not every dish is made with garlic.

Nearby attractions: Niton and Ventnor are pretty villages. Carisbrooke Castle and Osborne House are open to the public. Head to Brook Down and Compton Bay on the south-west coast for fantastic views.

Alternative campsite: Heathfield Farm (www.heathfieldcamping.co.uk, tel.: 01983 407822). A quiet site on the outskirts of Freshwater with sea views from some pitches.

Top Left: Campsite views of Brighstone Bay
Top Right: Wildflowers adorn the campsite
Bottom: VWs for hire from Isle of Wight Campers

South-West

Postern Hill
Wiltshire

Have you ever wondered why the stones at Avebury stone circle are all shaped inwards at the bottom? In theory, it's the smooth and delicate carving of a Neolithic labourer on these monsters of rock, but don't believe a word of it; it's sheep! These woolly beasts, fighting with an itch, use the stones as backscratchers, rubbing their lanolin coating onto the surface to reveal a well-worn, polished – diamond-shaped – monument.

Wiltshire, particularly around Marlborough, has an abundant supply of Neolithic monuments, hill forts and altogether unexplained goings-on. Close to the stone circle at Avebury is Silbury Hill, the largest man-made chalk mound in Europe, which is quite a claim to fame, even though no one really knows why it's there. Over the road is West Kennet Long Barrow, a burial chamber from an age that's far too long ago to even contemplate. And then there are the chalky figures that appear on the sides of prominent hills. There are more than ten white horses that dance and leap across the landscape around Wiltshire, making the county home to the largest population of hill figures in the country. Five of these are within 10 miles of Postern Hill campsite.

Postern Hill itself is situated above the pretty town of Marlborough in Savernake Forest, a 4,500-acre estate and the only forest still privately owned in Britain. It's an ancient woodland pre-dating the New Forest; oak trees with incredibly knobbly, wide girths are evident throughout. Henry VIII, of notable girth himself, used to visit to partake in a spot of stag hunting while staying at the estate's Tottenham House. There, having lopped off the head of his former wife, he eyed up the owner's daughter, one Jane Seymour. The rest, of course, is history. So, you never know, the very spot upon which you set up camp may well be the very place that King Henry stood to take aim at a red deer.

Above: Flowers are planted at the site to attract wildlife

Privately owned Savernake Forest is leased to the Forestry Commission and it's the Camping in the Forest arm that has set up camp at Postern Hill. They are brilliant at creating a totally natural atmosphere, with no set pitches; you park up on the grass, either under the trees or in the more open glade. There are hook-ups dotted about but, other than a 6-metre rule for fire safety, you can pitch your 'van anywhere you like.

Top Left: A sheep scratching itself against Avebury Stone Circle **Bottom Left:** Oak tree leaves – a prominent feature of Postern Hill

The beauty of the site is its simplicity. There's no enormous shower block to blot out the sun; in fact, there are no showers on site. The loos and washbasins, which are all incredibly clean, are housed in a very basic Portakabin. This may sound horrendous, but the Portakabin's dark-green colour blends in with the trees and is barely noticeable. Its exterior has been turned into a butterfly garden – the plants selected specifically to attract, with honeysuckle growing up the Portakabin and bee boxes attached to the wall.

Consideration of the natural habitat goes with the job for the wardens at Postern Hill and as a result they've managed to obtain a David Bellamy Gold Conservation Award for the work they do and a gold Green Tourism Award. Throughout the campsite there are little hideaways for birds, bees and creepy-crawlies; a display on the reception building tells you all about the different projects and the kinds of trees, birds and mammals that you're likely to spot. There's also information on how to keep a wildlife journal during your stay. They've also managed to double the amount of recycling that the campers do and in the loos there's information on saving water as well as light sensors to prevent wastage. Rainwater is also collected and used for watering the butterfly garden.

Savernake Forest is home to several species of bats and visitors can join an evening bat walk with a Forest Holidays' Ranger or take themselves on a self-guided tour armed with information from reception. Alternatively, the forest is there for walking or cycling, with cycle hire (including toddler options if you're coming with little ones) available in Marlborough. The town of Marlborough is accessible via a woodland footpath, 20 minutes down the hill.

Postern Hill Caravan and Camping Site

Marlborough, Wiltshire, SN8 4ND

01672 515195

www.campingintheforest.co.uk

Opening times: Open all year

Facilities: 170 pitches, hook-ups (though less electric points than pitches), toilets (no showers), battery charging, chemical toilet disposal point, cycle hire. Dogs welcome.

How to get there: A346, half a mile south of Marlborough. There is a little road noise at the campsite, but nothing too noticeable; you hear the birds more than the road. Pick a pitch farthest away (no hook-ups) and you won't hear it at all.

Food & drink: There is lots of choice in Marlborough. The Castle & Ball (tel.: 01672 515201), on the High Street, has a traditional beamed bar and a modern brasserie-style restaurant with great food. The Food Gallery (thefoodgallery.co.uk, tel.: 01672 514069) also has a great reputation for fabulous coffee and hot chocolate.

Nearby attractions: Avebury is 7 miles away and besides the circle, the village is very pretty and has a museum associated with the Neolithic monuments as well as a walled garden open to the public (NT), pub and shops. The Ridgeway Path begins at Avebury. Stonehenge is 20 miles from the site.

Alternative campsite: Brokerswood Country Park (www.brokerswood.net, tel.: 01373 822238). Half an hour's drive from Postern Hill, between Trowbridge and Westbury. A nice site that is slightly quieter than Postern Hill although the pitches are in rows with close proximity to one another. The neighbouring woodland, with its own fishing lake and activities, is accessible to campers and the entrance fee is included in the pitch price.

Top: Children climbing trees in Savernake Forest
Bottom Left: An Airstream caravan in the shelter at Postern Hill
Bottom Right: One of the conservation projects at Postern Hill

Riverside Lakes
Dorset

If there's one spot that truly sums up laid-back and chilled-out camping, Riverside Lakes has to be it. Respect for the owner's property and respect for your fellow campers are pretty much the only rules. And the campsite grounds are about as far removed from regimented as you can get.

There's a magical quality about Riverside Lakes. It's the kind of place where romance can blossom and marriage proposals are made, where even the ducks cement their relationships, blissfully happy with their waterside environment.

This is how campsites and caravan sites should be, a textbook model of easy-going solitude, where nature is queen and human life must fit in and adapt to what's around them.

You're never quite sure what to expect when you pull up at a campsite for the first time, although hopefully this book will address some of those apprehensions. When I first rolled up unannounced at Riverside Lakes, a group of people came tearing across the field to meet us – Tony with his wife and son, as it turned out. He stretched out a hand and then retracted it, 'Sorry, I can't shake your hand, we've been laying bark under the trees,' as the trio turned their hands over with a smile to reveal blackened palms. It could not have been a warmer welcome.

It was Tony and his family that, several years ago, dug a string of lakes and when some friends camped over for a party, comments were made about what a great spot it was. Riverside's first full season was 2009, after which Maggie and Nigel Richards took over the running of the site with their grown-up sons. Maggie and Nigel have retained the relaxed and very natural atmosphere, although that takes nothing away from the hard graft and attention to detail that shines through and creates a really pleasurable experience in what is, after all, their garden.

Above: A goose at Riverside Lakes

To describe it is almost to take away some of the magic – you do need to see it for yourself – but what was once a field is 'landscaped' so imaginatively that it appears entirely natural, as though the trees and

Left: Views across the lake from the campsite

the lakes have been there for eternity. Secret paths and bridges cut through the long grass, the kinds of paths that take you back to carefree childhood days when making grass dens was much more exciting than pollen counts. Each lake – there are three of them – has its own characteristics, attracting a different kind of wildlife. The first one is more open, the second is glade-like, while the third is wooded and entirely surrounded by trees, with an island providing a mini campsite for one. Above the lakes is an open field that just offers space, space to live and room to breathe.

After dark the campfires burn, large ones with log seats for communal storytelling or small ones for personal hand warmers. Forget heaters and comfy sofas in cosy 'vans, this is one place to live outdoors and watch the stars. Wood is delivered every night to your pitch in preparation for lighting a fire and drifting into another world as you watch the embers glow.

As the full moon rises and the braziers burn, solar-panelled lights glimmer faintly, marking the fairy trails to tread for a 'midnight' walk, to watch for bats, to listen to the sound of the geese skinny-dipping in the lakes, to hear the owl sing his midnight song – and to prepare a stick ready for a marshmallow. Yes, marshmallows are an absolute necessity. Ignore the dentist nagging your conscience and fetch out a toasting fork.

Not everyone will appreciate the symphonic tones of the dawn chorus, the resident geese not wishing to be outsung by the cuckoo. Most, however, find the Kune-Kune pigs adorable and the chickens perfect time-wasters as you watch their every move. Be prepared to do not a lot but sit and gaze in such a beautiful place.

Riverside Lakes

Slough Lane, Horton, Dorset, BH21 7JL

01202 821212

www.riversidelakes.co.uk

bookings@riversidelakes.co.uk

Opening times: End of April to end of September

Facilities: 5 pitches for caravans/motorhomes with hook-ups, showers and family bathroom, toilets, dishwashing area, recycling area, braziers and wood available, fishing by arrangement, glamping.

How to get there: Exit the A31 at the junction for Bournemouth A338 and Three Legged Cross. Follow the road through Three Legged Cross for approximately 6 miles. Riverside Lakes is down a private road on the right before entering the village of Horton.

Food & drink: Cranborne Stores (www.cranborne.co.uk) in the centre of Cranborne, and a part of the large Cranborne Estate, offers lots of tasty cheeses, deli items and home-made goodies, plus rare-breed meat from the estate, including venison and pheasant, and artisan breads made on the premises.

Nearby attractions: The New Forest is 6 miles away, with the small town of Ringwood a good starting point. Wimborne Minster is a very attractive town 10 miles from Riverside Lakes. The beaches of Poole and Bournemouth are a short drive. Moors Valley Country Park and Forest, along the same road as Riverside Lakes, has lots to offer.

Alternative campsite: Woolsbridge Manor Farm Caravan Park (www.woolsbridgemanorcaravanpark.co.uk, tel.: 01202 826369). On the same road 4 miles from Riverside Lakes at Three Legged Cross.

Top Left: Riverside Lakes Site
Bottom Left: The moon rises over Riverside Lakes
Right: Geese enjoying the lake

Corfe Castle
Dorset

Like so many fine English fortifications, Corfe Castle has had a grisly past. With tales of murder, deceit, captives and all-out war, its walls have seen many things too gruesome to contemplate, the worst of which must be the pilfering of its own stone for houses elsewhere.

Above: Hidden pitches on the campsite

Built when a millennium barely existed and William was conquering Europe, the castle became a part of royal history. Its defining moment came during the English Civil War when the Royalist stronghold took a battering from the Parliamentarians. Retreating after a botched attempt to take the castle resulted in a serious loss of life, Cromwell's men decided to have another go three years later, in 1646. This time, thanks to an insider betraying the ranks, the Royalist seat was not so strong; the castle was captured and blown up to prevent further occupation. Now, it's the tourists who besiege the ruined castle walls. Thankfully, the nearby campsite (franchised to the

Camping and Caravanning Club) half a mile away has a more peaceful outlook on life, where the only act of treason is performed by whoever ate the last bacon butty at breakfast unbeknown to the rest of the family in the privacy of their 'van.

Within ten minutes' walk of the castle, the campsite is found down a quiet country lane, set back from the road and surrounded by woodland. On the fringes of the site are pitches among the trees for those who fancy the wilder side of camping, while a central clearing takes the bulk of visitors. If there's one gripe, it's the usual thing of too many pitches pressed into one area at peak times, but there are no rules about parking your 'van to face a certain way, so the site has a good informal atmosphere, and with so many trees around to break up the woodland pitches, there's scope to escape people for those that want to. The facilities are immaculate in a well-maintained building with a pretty garden.

Corfe Castle – the campsite, the castle and the village – are on the Isle of Purbeck, which is a contravention of trade descriptions as it's no island, more a foot swinging around Poole Harbour to all but kick the cobwebs from the footballers' swanky homes on Sandbanks.

Running east to west of the peninsula are the Purbeck Hills, a ridge of chalky downs that, unlike Corfe Castle, the weak link in the chain, have kept many a marauding army from entering Britain. Ironically, it's the army that

Right: Corfe Castle

now uses much of the western ridge as a firing range. There are certain roads that take you through the range, such as the one from Corfe Castle to Lulworth Castle, a spookily quiet journey when the guns aren't blazing, with disconcerting road signs appealing to tank drivers to stick to the speed limits for tracked vehicles. The range is now considered an important nature reserve, and in the middle is the ghost village of Tyneham, the sad remains of a community that shut up shop in 1943 but which fully expected to breathe life into the old manor house, church and post office once again when the Second World War ended only to never be allowed to return. It too has an eerie presence of life standing still among the derelict buildings. Now a preserved museum, visitors can gain access at weekends and certain periods of the year, when the firing range is not in action; open gates to the range will determine if you can visit.

It's the Purbeck Hills that form the backdrop to the campsite and which are accessible through a private gate that joins the Purbeck Way, a footpath that bumps along the spine of the ridge and commands excellent views of the Jurassic coastline, a World Heritage Site. There's a footpath directly from the site to the castle as well and into the very pretty but tourist-magnet village where there are a smattering of hostelries, tea rooms and gift shops in which to while away an afternoon.

Castles with a little less history – and considerably less chance of making one – can be built at the Blue Flag beaches of Swanage and Studland. They're popular haunts but you don't have to join the queue for the car parks. Leaving the car or motorhome in the campsite, you can roll up your beach towel and use it as a headrest for the 6-mile journey by steam. Chugging along the tracks behind an ancient locomotive on the Swanage Railway, reaching the beach in the way our Victorian forefathers did, certainly beats sitting behind the wheel of a car.

Corfe Castle Camping and Caravanning Club Site

Bucknowle, Wareham, Dorset, BH20 5PQ

01929 480280

www.campingandcaravanningclub.co.uk

Opening times: March to October

Facilities: 80 pitches, hook-ups, hot showers, family showers, disabled facilities, dishwashing, laundry, small site shop, gas exchange, dogs welcome. Chocks and levellers required.

How to get there: A351 Wareham to Swanage road. With the Visitor Centre on your left, turn right immediately in front of the castle ruins towards Church Knowle. The site is half a mile farther on the right.

Food & drink: The Bankes Arms Hotel (www.bankesarms.com, tel.: 01929 450225) in the village of Corfe Castle is a beautiful old building with a lovely garden overlooking the castle. Attractive, though not cheap, menu. An alternative is The New Inn (www.newinn-churchknowle.co.uk, tel.: 01929 480357) at neighbouring Church Knowle, offering menus with local, seasonal produce.

Nearby attractions: Lulworth Castle and Cove, with the arching Durdle Door, are 6 miles from the site, crossing the army range. The Tank Museum and Monkey World are just west of Wareham, an attractive gateway town to the Isle of Purbeck. Brownsea Island, the birthplace of the scouting movement and a spectacular nature reserve with red squirrels, can be accessed from Swanage.

Alternative campsite: Knitson Farm (www.knitsonfarm.co.uk). A quiet farm site down a narrow lane in the middle of nowhere but close to Swanage, with lovely views of the hills. No hook-ups.

Top Left: The footpath leading to Corfe Castle
Top Right: Views over the village of Corfe Castle and the Purbeck Hills
Bottom: Wildflowers fill the campsite with colour

Burrowhayes Farm
Somerset

Noon, and the sun hangs poised, slowly roasting the lower slopes; the horizon, filled with a sultry haze, clears to reveal higher peaks and a sky fit for adventure. The alpacas trip in line along the hard-trodden path, accompanied by their masters and a posse of trekkers. Welcome to the Andes. Sorry, make that Exmoor: the lower slopes being the foot of Black Hill, the trees the thickening forest at Dunster, the masters Cathy and Rod and the alpacas Rolo and Polo.

Above: The bridge at Burrowhayes Farm

Cathy and Rod run a small farm and Exmoor Owl and Hawk Centre at Allerfod (www.exmoorfalconry.co.uk) within the National Park. Besides their falconry experiences, they take punters on alpaca walks through the beautiful Exmoor countryside.

Of course, Exmoor is traditionally known for a different kind of trekking, the beautiful moorland scenery lending itself to pony rides through the open countryside. One place to trot towards is Burrowhayes Farm, run by Julian and Marion Dascombe. Their family has lived on the farm, close to Dunster and owned by the National Trust, for over 60 years, and when dairy farming declined some years ago they set up other projects, including a campsite and riding stables.

To say that the location is 'pretty' would be timid. Set within the 12,500-acre Holnicote Estate, also owned by the National Trust, the farm has ancient woodland, sheep in green pastures and a few folk from the tiny hamlet of Horner for its neighbours. A little packhorse bridge marks your arrival at the campsite, allowing pixies to cross the small stream that runs through the farm. Caravans and motorhomes can pitch up next to the stream, the soothing sound of the gurgling waters melting away the stresses of a hectic life. In a long strip, following the line of the river valley, the campsite continues towards woodlands, with further pitches, a few static caravans for hire and a grassy knoll for tents. The woods then line the lower slopes of the hillside that shelters campers from the easterly winds on the south-facing site – behind are the magnificent Moors and Dunkery Beacon rising up sharply and creating a backdrop that's worthy of several nights' stay.

Right: The Horner Water runs past Burrowhayes Farm

The riding stables are right next to the campsite, with horses and ponies suitable for all riders, including those that have never slipped a foot into a stirrup before. There are escorted rides through the Horner valley and up onto the moorland, where views of the Exmoor coastline will take the rider's breath away. Novices really need to be at least nine years old to take part in one of the escorted rides, but for little ones who like the idea of the saddle, there are half-hour treks on suitably small ponies with the reins held by an adult.

If taking to the saddle is simply not your thing, it's essential to find some other way to see the estate, it being so varied and rich in landscape and wildlife: stand still for a moment on the top of Dunkery Beacon, Exmoor's highest point, and you may catch a glimpse of the red deer that inhabit the heather. In fact, you'll probably find that, unless a rainstorm is visually sweeping its way side-on towards the hill, one moment is not enough to take in the views, which on even the haziest of days include the outline of the Welsh coast.

Close by, Dunkery and Horner Woods National Nature Reserve is home to a vast collection of ancient oaks, along with several species of bats. Hang around at dusk and you may be lucky to see one at a time when they're not hanging around.

Sometimes, though, the best way to see the countryside is without moving anything other than the muscles required to spread a scone with some thick clotted cream and raise a cup of tea to the lips. The intensely beautiful village of Selworthy or Porlock, both a matter of minutes by car or bike from the campsite, are a good place to partake in such an activity. Then again, you may prefer to sample the Porlock Bay Oysters, reintroduced to the area in 2015 and right on the doorstep of the campsite. They're only available, at present, in local restaurants and are regarded as the finest in England.

Burrowhayes Farm

West Luccombe, Porlock, Minehead, Somerset,
TA24 8HT

01643 862463

www.burrowhayes.co.uk

info@burrowhayes.co.uk

Opening times: Mid-March to end of October

Facilities: 54 pitches with and without hook-ups, including 6 fully-serviced hardstanding, static caravans for hire, free hot showers and toilets in clean amenity building, chemical toilet disposal point, dishwashing, laundry, well-stocked shop, riding stables.

How to get there: A39 Bridgwater to Barnstaple road. Five miles west of Minehead, just before Porlock, turn left, signed Horner. Site is straight ahead after half a mile.

Food & drink: Periwinkle Tea Rooms (tel: 01643 863341), housed in a thatched cottage at Selworthy Green and within the Holnicote Estate, is a must for cream teas.

Nearby attractions: Porlock is a small town with a very pretty olde-worlde high street with lots of places to eat and a few gift shops. Porlock Weir is the place to reach the sea, but for an old-fashioned seaside resort, make for Minehead, Butlins and all. For fabulous views of the coast on foot climb Selworthy Beacon or in the car (or small motorhome) take the coastal toll road from Porlock.

Alternative campsite: Halse Farm (see page 179, www.halsefarm.co.uk, tel.: 01643 851259). Next to Winsford Hill in the heart of Exmoor and with superb views, half an hour's drive from Burrowhayes Farm.

Left: Horseriding from the campsite
Top Right: Spring primroses line the entranceway
Bottom Right: Burrowhayes Farm

Top Left: One of the two lodges in the park **Bottom Left:** Tree-covered pitches in 'The Arc' at Alpine Grove

Alpine Grove Park
Somerset

Forget the Wright Brothers, John Stringfellow of Chard got there first. The town's claim to fame, apart from being Somerset's most southerly town, is thanks to Mr Stringfellow, who in 1848, some half a century before the Wright brothers' 'first' powered flight, built and flew a powered aeroplane in a disused lace-making factory in the town. The contraption admittedly only made a few feet of progress but, nevertheless, it happened.

Chard's more recent claim to fame, at least for caravanners, is being home to the wonderful Alpine Grove. As its name describes, it's a woodland park, but with a history. If you lift your head skywards while you're sat by your 'van sampling the delights of a summer barbecue, it's impossible not to notice how tall and straight the oak trees around you are, the lower branches all but vanished, the crowns lifted. Allegedly, the woodland was created as a shipbuilding plantation in the days when boats looked like boats and men took to the high seas trading spices and exploring new lands – and when Dorset and south Somerset had a mammoth shipbuilding industry. Crewkerne made the sails, Bridport made the ropes and Lyme Regis, a mere 9 log-hauling miles from Chard, made the boats. Of course, oak is renowned for being a slow grower and by the time the handsome beauties in the campsite today had grown to any useable size, steel had become the norm and these poor specimens were redundant. Still, for those who like to camp among the trees and listen to the owl hoot at bedtime, we can only be grateful for the birth of steel.

Alpine Grove is organized in two connected sections. In front of Richard and Helen Gurd's eco-friendly house is the more open oak wood, 'The Arc', where light filters through onto a large gravel area and several grass lawns that, in the sunshine, feel like a Mediterranean garden. In fact, part of it is their garden, a roped off area with the finest of hitches where their own children can have as normal a life as is possible with the comings and goings of everybody else's kids. There's a choice of hard standing and grass pitches, but it's all very relaxed and you can choose how you like to set up your 'van. Sprawled everywhere are the exploding blooms of rhododendrons; nothing is too twee. Slightly farther back from the gravel garden is the denser woodland, where pitches are in between birch and oak trees and a jungle of rhododendron bushes – a truly magnificent site that would give the Lost Gardens of Heligan a run for its money. Light still comes through the trees, but there's a definite sense of being able to lose yourself in the wood. There are a few hook-ups in the deeper woods, but most of the 'pitches' in that area are without electricity.

Also in these woods are two log cabins, tucked among the trees, where, when the campers have gone home to prepare for the following year's adventures, guests can strike a match to the log-burning stove and snuggle down as if it were a long Scandinavian winter with the snow deep and crisp and even. Both cabins are kitted out for your every need, including an alfresco balcony for the English summers.

Facing Right: A path leading into the woods at Alpine Grove

Living under the trees, it's inevitable that ecology and caring for the environment is at the heart of the campsite, with all kinds of measures in place: creating habitats for birds and animals (look out for the owl box in the woods), harvesting rainwater (there's a 'submarine'-sized tank underground), which is filtered to fill the small swimming pool, using an economical heat exchanger to warm the pool, using home-made compost from the woodland leaves and providing local produce in the on-site shop.

Above: Rhododendrons are a major feature in the park

Part of Richard's aim is to ensure that when children leave the site they know a little bit more about the environment than upon their arrival. He's created a scavenger trail whereby children have to find different natural objects in exchange for a prize – so if they arrive not knowing what an oak leaf looks like, they certainly will do by the time they leave. They'll also learn what an oak log looks like – and discover what a toasted marshmallow tastes like. Richard hires out braziers for the evening, complete with lots of wood, local sausages, marshmallows and a set of toasting forks specially made by the village blacksmith. Just remember a marshmallow in the mouth can feel as hot as the blacksmith's furnace.

Alpine Grove Woodland Park

Forton, Near Chard, Somerset, TA20 4HD

01460 63479

www.alpinegrovetouringpark.com

stay@alpinegrovetouringpark.com

Opening times: Easter to end of September (camping), all year (log cabins)

Facilities: 40 pitches, hook-ups (though less hook-ups than pitches), free hot showers, family/disabled bathroom with a half-bath, chemical toilet disposal point, laundry room, dishwashing area, small heated swimming pool, children's trampoline and slide, gas exchange, shop selling local produce, recycling facilities, free herb garden for cooks! Dogs welcome.

How to get there: From A303, take the A30 (from the south-west) or A358 (from Ilminster) to Chard. Follow B3162 for 2 miles. Turn right just after the village of Forton (at brown campsite sign). Campsite is 150 metres farther on the left.

Food & drink: The Golden Fleece (www.thegoldenfleecechard .co.uk, tel.: 01460 220285), South Chard, is within a mile of the campsite and walking distance across the fields; serves 'traditional' fare, there's quite a lot 'with chips' but it fills you up. Known for being accommodating towards food allergies.

Nearby attractions: Lyme Regis and the Jurassic Coast are 9 miles from the site. The south Devon coast (Branscombe, Seaton) is within striking distance too. Cricket St Thomas and Forde Abbey are 2 miles away. Spectacular countryside is all around!

Alternative campsite: The Golden Fleece (www.thegoldenfleecechard.co.uk, tel.: 01460 220285). The aforementioned pub has a straightforward campsite on the adjacent field.

Halse Farm
Somerset

If a house was painted pastel pink or yellow in an inner-city setting, in all likelihood it would be condemned by passers-by as tacky and tasteless. Put a pastel pink or yellow house into certain rural areas, though, top it with a thatch bonnet and allow a complementary coloured rose to ramble up its front wall and we all flock to see it, commenting on its prettiness and old-world charm before buying a box of clotted cream fudge with a picture of said houses on the lid.

Somerset is one such country to be blessed with these objects of desire and nowhere more so than in Exmoor National Park. The village of Winsford is full of the picturesque lime-washed higgledy-piggledy cottages with cream tea offerings and a feeling of life passing by at an altogether slower pace.

Halse Farm, a mile from Winsford, is also yellow, painted in the traditions of the area. It's a working sheep and beef farm, and the animals can be seen grazing in the fields around the campsite. The site is all very basic and unpretentious – deliberately so – where visitors can experience the tranquillity that makes Exmoor so different to the tourist traps of neighbouring Devon. It is without games rooms or restaurants and bars, rather there is open space standing by ready for a Frisbee to be thrown or a shuttlecock to feel the force of a racket. With the peace comes the sound of birdsong; the site has

won the David Bellamy Gold Conservation Award for several years, and has all kinds of ideas in place to encourage wildlife. There are hook-ups in one field, while another is left for 'wild' camping, but both overlook the moorland. With such open ground and little shade, sun worshippers will be fine; shade lovers might like to make sure the awning is in tip-top shape.

Above: Sheepdog at Halse Farm

Where the moorland stops, the green valleys take over, each horizon of hills overlapping the next, merging somewhere in the distance, the hedgerows carving up the meadows into hotchpotch squares. To go walking – or riding – is as simple as putting one step in front of another with the whole of Exmoor under your boot or hoof. The moor is interlaced with footpaths and bridleways and the good folk at Halse Farm have come up with half a dozen circular walks from the campsite, based upon their exceedingly good knowledge of the local area. Being so close (across the road), Winsford Hill is a good place to start and also the place to see wild Exmoor ponies, classified as an endangered breed by the Rare Breeds Survival Trust. There are very few left on the Moors, as the breed nearly became extinct when Exmoor was used as a military training ground during the Second World War.

When it's time to set the feet tapping to a different tune, the Tarr Steps would make a notable song. They're more a kind of stepping stone across the River Barle, an impressive clapper bridge made with gigantic slabs of stone resting upon one another and spanning 50 metres over the water. Or, for walking with a sense of purpose, the Coleridge Way covers 51 miles of up and down countryside across parts of Exmoor and North Somerset from Lynmouth to Nether Stowey in the Quantock Hills. Nether Stowey was the one-time home of the poet Samuel Taylor Coleridge, where he wrote many of his famous poems, including 'The Rime of the Ancient Mariner' and 'Kubla Khan'. His house, owned by the National Trust, is open to the public.

For a true jewel, the village of Dunster is sure to have you reaching for the camera with its cobbled streets and the fabulously crooked yarn market building in the village centre. The place is a time warp, with the beautiful castle keeping watch high on the hill above, its sub-tropical garden confusing visitors of being in some distant land rather than overlooking the Bristol Channel. The village does nothing other than be Dunster, the product of being a very pretty village for a tourist industry where eateries and gift shops line the streets, waiting to entice visitors to part with their holiday money. Motorhomes will find easy parking in the large car park just north of the village by the National Park Visitor Centre.

Halse Farm

Winsford, Exmoor, Somerset, TA24 7JL

01643 851259

www.halsefarm.co.uk

brown@halsefarm.co.uk

Opening times: Mid-March to end of October

Facilities: 22 pitches with hook-ups (half of which are on hardstandings), free hot showers, toilets in heated, refurbished building, chemical toilet disposal point, disabled facilities, baby-changing facilities, shaver points, laundry, dishwashing, gas exchange, play area, information room, wi-fi. Dogs welcome.

How to get there: From A356 Minehead to Tiverton road, turn, signed Winsford. In village turn left/bear left past Royal Oak Inn. Site is up the hill, 1 mile from pub on left, just after the cattle grid. Avoid very narrow route through Dulverton.

Food & drink: The Royal Oak Inn (www.royaloakexmoor.co.uk, tel.: 01643 851455) in Winsford, 1 mile from site, is a lovely thatched pub full of character, with great food.

Nearby attractions: For another jewel-like village filled with classic painted houses, head to Dulverton, 5 miles south of Halse Farm. It, like Dunster, is a miniature tourist mecca (large 'vans will struggle with the narrow lane into the village).

Alternative campsite: Wimbleball Lake (www.outdoorandactive .uk.com/camping/wimbleball-lake/, tel.: 01398 371460). Peaceful campsite in a park next to Wimbleball Lake, with lots of walks and wildlife.

Top Left: Views across the campsite from Winsford Hill
Top Right: Heather at Halse Farm
Bottom: Wild Exmoor ponies grazing on the hill

Bolberry House Farm and Karrageen Devon

When there are hundreds of campsites and touring parks along the British coast, each one promoting a 'beautiful sea view', how do you choose one? More so, how do I select out of the hundreds for inclusion in this book?

Above: Views from Bolberry House Farm

Well, one that actually has a sea view is a good start (some are a little shy of the truth). Then one that is also surrounded by some superb countryside, that's blissfully quiet without feeling the need to maintain silence yourself, and where the welcome is as warm as your duvet. If you get all these things, then you've found a site that's really worth staying at. Actually, I found two within a couple of hundred yards of one another and, hard-pressed to choose between the pair, I decided not to.

South Devon is a web of tiny narrow lanes with claustro-phobically high hedges. Karrageen and Bolberry House

Farm are down one of these lanes, poked into a corner of the county where the bright lights of big town life don't shine and a slower pace is altogether invigorating. The lane very gradually falls to the sea at Hope Cove, a mile on from the campsites, where you'll find a gaggle of attractive thatched cottages, cosy cafes and a sheltered beach snuggled between the imposing rocks and caves.

Both campsites are similar in nature, in that they are grass fields with numbered pitches but no defined markings or hardstanding. Neither has the trappings of bars, laid-on entertainment or major facilities.

Karrageen is the farthest to reach, being 200 yards farther down the lane. Its sloping field is terraced and broken up by hedges, so visitors can choose to stay at the top of the site – where most 'vans congregate to reach the best views – or tucked away in a more secluded spot in between the trees. Behind the touring area there's a field of mobile homes run by the same family, which are hidden behind another tall South Devon hedge. Well thought out, the leafy partitions in the camping field are not in dead-straight lines, so the site has the feeling of being totally natural with lots of space.

Fiona, who runs Bolberry House Farm with her sister, is a real people person. She describes their campsite as a village green, where people 'live' around the edges leaving space in the middle for ball games and kite-flying, without the need to send the children off to some

Right: The stunning coast of Bolberry Down

far-flung corner to play, although there is a small play area in the corner and families can pitch close by. Being a little higher up than Karrageen, the views of Bigbury Bay and the rolling countryside, full of sheep and lovely brown Devon cows, are just as fine, but the site also has views of Dartmoor, hazily disappearing into the distance. The campsite has been run by Fiona's family for generations, and I met a man staying with his children who has been coming to the site since he was a little nipper himself; his parents were there, too, and it's this family atmosphere with traditional values that keep the campsite special.

A second field, 'The Paddock' is a little farther down the hill and is used mainly by tents with a few 'van pitches. A grassy footpath across the field connects the two camping areas – also used as a dog walk – allowing top-field campers to call at the owner's house if required.

However, there's no gain without pain and you do have to negotiate the narrow, high-hedged lane to access both sites. Karrageen has a chicane bend added for good measure. These may not be the best sites for really nervous drivers (or those hopeless at reversing), but Fiona at Bolberry House Farm will escort you from the main road to her site should you require it and if you pick your timing for arrivals and exits, everything will be fine and dandy. As ever, the road always seems wider on the way out and you'll wonder why you made such a fuss on arrival.

After all the pain you will be rewarded with those 'beautiful sea views', as well as great countryside and some lovely walking territory. The South West Coast Path can be accessed a fraction of a mile away at Bolberry Down, an incredible stretch of coastline looking in the opposite direction (towards Bolt Head) to the campsites' views. Karrageen and Bolberry House Farm really are at the tip of South Devon.

Bolberry House Farm

Bolberry, Marlborough, Kingsbridge,
South Devon, TQ7 3DY

01548 561251

www.bolberryparks.co.uk

enquiries@bolberryparks.co.uk

Karrageen

Bolberry, Marlborough, Kingsbridge,
South Devon, TQ7 3EN

01548 561230

www.karrageen.co.uk

phil@karrageen.co.uk

Opening times: Bolberry: Easter to October
Karrageen: Beginning of April to end of September

Facilities: Bolberry: Pitches with and without hook-ups, static caravans for hire, hot showers, toilets, dishwashing, laundry, play area, log cabin shop selling local BBQ produce and basic camping kit (high season). Dogs welcome.
Karrageen: Pitches with hook-ups, static caravans for hire, hot showers and toilets in recently refurbished amenity block with eco-friendly solar heating, disabled/family shower room, chemical toilet disposal point, dishwashing, licensed shop with fresh bread and fresh-baked breakfast goodies. Dogs welcome.

How to get there: Bolberry: From A38, turn onto A3121, signed Kingsbridge. Two miles past Aveton Gifford, turn right onto B3197, then A381, signed Salcombe. In Malborough turn right (tight turn) and follow the brown camping signs. Bolberry House Farm is 2 miles, along on the right. Road is very narrow from Malborough.
Karrageen: Shortly after Bolberry House, also on the right.

Food & drink: Numerous choices including The Cove Cafe Bar (www.thecovedevon.co.uk, tel: 01548 561376) in Hope Cove and the Walkers' Hut at East Soar Farm (www.eastsoar outdoorexperience.co.uk) for delicious Aga-baked cakes.

Nearby attractions: The beautiful town of Salcombe straddles the Kingsbridge Estuary; try some Salcombe Dairy ice cream.

Alternative campsite: Bolberry: Karrageen. Simple!
Karrageen: Bolberry. Simple!

Top Left: Karrageen campsite **Bottom Left:** The playground at Bolberry House Farm **Right:** Sunset over the sea at Bolberry House Farm

Napps
Devon

North Devon, it seems, without physically counting, plays host to more campsites and caravan parks per square inch than any other county. Many are squeezed into the area west of Exmoor National Park and north of the River Taw, with the coast from Ilfracombe to Westward Ho! being the main attraction. Many of them are also all-singing, all-dancing theme parks, with row upon row of static caravans more compact than a tin of pilchards and where the touring area is usually tagged onto the end as a bit of an afterthought.

Not so at Napps. Napps is solely for touring caravans and motorhomes and a few tents. The owners, the Richards family, actually manage it themselves rather than have somebody else in charge. What's more, they've owned it for a very long time, as it was once a farm that has gradually changed into the touring park it is today. There are still elements of the farm about, notably the sheep that graze among the yellow gorse bushes on the hill behind the site. It occupies 40 acres, most of which is taken up to provide comfortably large pitches for the tourers, while the remainder is woodland and a small area used to house the amenities and a great swimming pool.

Many sites claim to be right on the coast when actually they're some way (often miles) back; Napps genuinely is coastal and in a designated Area of Outstanding Natural Beauty. The site sits on top of the cliffs at Watermouth Cove and has the quiet Broadsands beach a mere 200 yards from the site. This is a small, sheltered beach that's safe for bathing and for casting a line from the rocks in the hope of catching a fish supper. The views of the sea are magnificent and, depending on where you pitch or go for a little wander, there are different parts of the coast to see. Most pitches look out over Watermouth Cove, with Broadsands beach hidden from view at the foot of the cliffs, but wander to the far side of the site and there are more vistas along the

Above: Sheep at Napps

coastline to Combe Martin Bay and, from time to time, dolphins, porpoises and seals are spotted in the sea. While many of the sites in the area are close to the roadside, this campsite is well away from the traffic, with its own private drive and woodland obscuring any sight or sound of passing cars. This means that wildlife love the site, as do the guests, who return year after year, with a resident pair of buzzards soaring overhead and badgers making occasional nocturnal appearances.

The site has been carefully landscaped and terraced so that everyone gets the benefit of the views and the orange glow of the sea as the sun sets across the water. Trees planted here and there break up the long lines of the terraces but not so many as to spoil anyone's view and there are palms to give it a distinctive Riviera feeling. Each terrace provides sufficient flat space to spread out before the next drop down the hill. For caravanners fed up with being blamed for clogging up the M5, the campsite offers a summer parking facility to leave the 'van on site throughout the high season.

The South West Coast Path trips right past the entrance to the site, but for those quite happy to leave the associated blisters of covering the full 630-mile trail (it's the longest National Trail in the country) to someone else, it's nevertheless a handy way of reaching Ilfracombe (remembering it's uphill on the return) or for reaching other beaches along the coast.

While Ilfracombe looks to be in urgent need of a facelift, Exmoor National Park begins just round the corner at Combe Martin Bay and there's a swathe of lesser-known countryside just inland to explore when everyone else is tearing towards the beach and picking sand from their ice cream. Lynton, on the hill, and Lynmouth, down by the sea, are connected by the cliff railway and have both retained the quaint charm of villages caught in a past world. However, don't make this excursion on your way home with the caravan attached, as there are steep hills and hairpin bends to rival Alpine roads.

When it all gets too hot for putting on a pair of walking boots, exchange them for a pair of flip-flops and lie out by the pool back at the campsite – it's what's called armchair travelling.

Napps Touring Park

Old Coast Road, Berrynarbor, North Devon, EX34 9SW

01271 882557

www.napps.co.uk

info@napps.fsnet.co.uk

Opening times: Beginning of March to end of October

Facilities: 114 grass and hardstanding pitches (plus a tent field), hook-ups, free hot showers, family washrooms, toilets, dishwashing, laundry, recycling area, chemical toilet disposal point, heated swimming and paddling pools, tennis court, playground, on-site shop, bar and bistro with sea-view terrace, games room. Dogs welcome.

How to get there: From A361, turn onto A399, signed for Combe Martin and Ilfracombe. Two miles after Combe Martin, the site is along a private drive on the right, just before the Sawmill Inn. Avoid travelling through Barnstaple as it has long delays, even out of peak season.

Food & drink: The Old Sawmills Inn (tel.: 01271 883388) is within walking distance, on the road close to the entrance to Napps. It's a family pub with children allowed everywhere and a reasonably priced, extensive menu. Ye Old Globe Inn (tel.: 01271 882465), half a mile away in the village of Berrynarbor, is full of character.

Nearby attractions: Watersmeet, close to Lynton, is a great place for a walk, with dramatic gorges and waterfalls hidden in ancient woodlands.

Alternative campsite: Watermouth Cove Holiday Park (www.watermouthcoveholidays.co.uk, tel.: 01271 862504). Below Napps, right on the cove and next to the small marina. It has its own private beach and stretch of coastline, plus three caves to explore. There's sea-worthy kayak hire too. Some road noise.

Top Left: Views of the North Devon coast from Napps
Top Right: Widmouth Head
Bottom: Hele Bay, near Napps

North Morte Farm
Devon

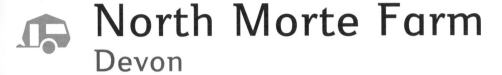

At first sight one could be forgiven for dismissing North Morte Farm as being an all-static site. On second glance it tells a different story – one that needs explaining.

The site is positioned along a no-through road on the outskirts of Mortehoe, a traditional village on a North Devon cliff top with a few houses, shops and pubs clustered together, and somewhere for a cream tea.

Much of the campsite, the part you're first greeted with, is an area of tidy but abundant static holiday homes, a sight that, but for the narrowness of the approach road, would potentially have you considering a swift U-turn. But venture beyond this and the story changes and, it would seem, the whole world opens out. Behind these static caravans a small touring area sits. It's sheltered from the coastal winds behind a hedge, which also blocks the view of the statics, and is peacefully quiet. With the farm adjoining National Trust land, there is some superb North Devon scenery to look at opposite and the pitches closest to the amenity building also get the best views of the sea. Of the 35 grass and hardstanding pitches, a few are taken up by seasonal 'vans, but there is plenty of room for tourers and bookings are taken for this area.

However, if you continue even farther into the campsite, through the gate, moving away from the statics and the official touring area, the scene changes again – to one of unrefined beauty, where every natural fold and crease of the earth is a part of the campsite and where your contemplation of the terrain is interrupted by sharp intakes of air at the prospect of the seascape. These fields – with ups and downs that correspond with the peaks and troughs of the tide, nooks and crannies, secret hidey-holes and ledges, all interspersed with windswept trees leaning inland and hedges of gorse and bracken – make up the 'Camping Area'. Owing to planning regulations, caravans are not allowed onto the camping fields but motorhomes are. There are no designated pitches and no bookings taken on this particular part of the campsite – you just turn

Above: Sunset over North Morte Farm

up. With the exception of the summer holidays, it's rarely full with such a large area. The fields slope down towards the cliff's edge so everyone has a good sight of the glorious sunsets that drop down dramatically over the west-facing coastline, the sun appearing to melt into the sea. There are lots of flat spots but ramps will generally be required on at least one wheel.

Rockham Beach can be accessed from the site, a sharpish 500-yard walk down the cliff face. A mixture of sand and craggy rocks, it stays relatively quiet because of the tricky access but its rock pools practically hand out prawns for anyone with a makeshift net in need of a seafood supper.

Far away from the heaving masses and bustling Blue Flag beaches further south, this is Devon at its finest and most remote, where, despite it being one of the most popular camping counties during the summer, you can still find yourself alone, especially if you take advantage of the campsite's early and late seasons in April or October, when all but the hardiest of tent campers have stayed at home.

Heading left out of the campsite entrance, you can follow the footpath to Bull Point, where the Bristol Channel ends and the Atlantic delivers all its power and glory, the rocks taking the punishing blows with significant strength. A lighthouse forewarns passing sailors of the dangers that lie beneath and with good reason; many an ancient mariner met his final moments around this shoreline, with only one place more fearsome to a sailing ship – Morte Point, the finger that picked off more sailors of old than anywhere else along the coast. Its jagged rocks simulate a miniature ridge of Dolomites and hold a beauty that has to be respected. Walkers can tread this in a circular walk from the campsite, which takes in elements of the South West Coast Path and the Tarka Trail. Other footpaths and cycleways that make up the Tarka Trail, based upon the imaginary route taken by the fictional otter in Henry Williamson's famous book *Tarka the Otter*, are also close by.

North Morte Farm Caravan and Camping Park

Mortehoe, Woolacombe, North Devon, EX34 7EG

01271 870381

www.northmortefarm.co.uk

info@northmortefarm.co.uk

Opening times: End of March to end of October

Facilities: 35 touring pitches with hook-ups for caravans and motorhomes, large camping area for motorhomes and tents without hook-ups, static caravans for hire, hot showers, toilets, chemical toilet disposal point, dishwashing, laundry, shop, play area, gas exchange, wi-fi. Dogs welcome.

How to get there: A361, signed Ilfracombe. Ten miles from Barnstaple, at Mullacott Cross roundabout, turn left, signed Mortehoe and Woolacombe. In 2 miles, turn right, signed Mortehoe. In Mortehoe village, turn right, signposted to Bull Point Lighthouse. Site is 500 yards farther on the left, on a narrow lane.

Food & drink: Miss Fea's Cafe (www.thesmugglersrest.co.uk, tel.: 01271 870891) in North Morte and within a short walk of the campsite. Opened in 2016 following an extensive refurbishment of an old village property, this is the place to eat in the vicinity.

Nearby attractions: Morte Bay is one of the finest swimming beaches in the area, as is Saunton Sands. Croyde Bay is the renowned surfing beach for North Devon.

Alternative campsite: Warcombe Farm (www.warcombefarm.co.uk, tel.: 01271 870690). A lovely 'inland' campsite 2 miles from Mortehoe with lots of facilities, a fishing lake and superb amenities; sea views from some areas of the site.

Left: Hiking along the coastline from North Morte Farm
Top Right: Open space pitches for motorhomes and campervans
Bottom Right: A Devonshire stone wall topped with grape hyacinths

Tristram
Cornwall

Never mind **Surfin' USA** and open-top cabriolets, the good vibrations are in Cornwall. Surfing allegedly originated in Polynesia and was brought to British shores by the one and only Captain James Cook. It's rumoured that when the Hawaiian natives hit the waves all those years ago, they did it naked. Mercifully, the Brits show a little more modesty – at least they do in Polzeath. Either that or it's too damned cold and the possibility of hypothermia setting in is enough to avoid baring all.

Above: Surfers at Polzeath

Polzeath, as is usual in Cornwall, was once a sleepy little village minding its own business on the north shore. Then, a few wave-catchers found it and were impressed by the swell coming off the Atlantic. Now it's global, with surfers from around the world donning a wetsuit or a pair of boardshorts, and one of the biggest surf schools, Surf's Up (www.surfsupsurfschool.com) has its HQ there. What's particularly nice about Polzeath, though, is that,

while every other person is a surfer, shops still sell buckets, spades and beach balls too, with the main beach attracting a throng of families looking to build the finest motte and bailey – temporarily. It's an eclectic mix.

Within a longboard length of the beach in, arguably, the best position in town is Tristram. It may sound like the hip name of a surfer, but Tristram is actually a campsite. On the hill behind it is a not-so-impressive row of houses, but it's not difficult to guess which way punters will point their 'van, considering that the site overlooks the bay, the beach and across to the next headland.

The campsite is well and truly geared up for surfers; as well as the usual clean and tidy shower block, there's somewhere to wash wetsuits and the reception hires out equipment. But you don't have to be in with the crowd to enjoy Tristram, because the location alone is worth a visit. So while some are waxing down their surfboards, others can wax lyrical about the views.

The site is gently sloping so everyone benefits from the panorama, with a dozen premier pitches on terraced ground closest to the beach, commanding the best views and the most money. It's split into three fields, one used mostly for tents, the other two for 'vans, divided by fencing and containing hook-ups with the amenity building conveniently in the centre so no one has to walk too far after a hard day trying to stay upright. The Cracking Crab Beach Cafe is adjacent

Right: The stunning view from the site.

to the site, too, with an equally cracking garden that overlooks the beach and the cliffs and serving a great selection of fresh seafood.

There's a private entrance to the fine golden sands and the South West Coastal Path, which runs right past the site, giving easy access for all into the village but also to walkers and cyclists looking for a bracing journey along the rugged cliffs. Alternative beaches can be reached this way, too. Head north and there are lots of tiny coves to explore before reaching Pentire Point and on to Port Quin and Port Isaac. Go south for Greenaway beach, full of rock pools, for a spot of crabbing, or Daymer Bay to test out some new waves. Keep moving towards Rock and you can catch a ferry over to Padstow to sample Rick Stein's fare at his Seafood Restaurant or simply sit on the quayside with an open wrapper of fish and chips, listening to the sound of the gulls.

St Enodoc, just south of Polzeath, boasts two golf courses both belonging to the same club, where day visitors are welcome to tee off; the courses are reputed to provide the best golf in the south-west. St Enodoc is also known for being the final resting place of one-time Poet Laureate Sir John Betjeman, who lived in the nearby village of Trebetherick. He had a lifelong love of north Cornwall, often referring to it in his poetry. The John Betjeman Centre, located in the old railway station at Wadebridge, houses a memorabilia room dedicated to the popular poet, with various items on display.

Wadebridge is also on the Camel Trail, a 17-mile-long cycle way (also used by walkers and horseriders) from Padstow to Bodmin that utilizes the old disused railway for traffic-free pedalling. It's beautifully flat so not too much exertion is required, and, if refreshment is required along the way, why not stop off at the celebrity-chef endorsed Camel Valley Vineyard for a glass of English wine and a guided tour of the vines. Cheers!

Tristram Camping Park

Polzeath, Wadebridge, Cornwall, PL27 6UG

01208 862215

www.polzeathcamping.co.uk

info@tristramcampsite.co.uk

Opening times: March to October

Facilities: 100 pitches, hook-ups, modern showers, toilets, laundry, chemical toilet disposal point, wetsuit wash room, wetsuit and surf equipment hire, private access to beach, cafe adjacent, wi-fi. Dogs welcome (the beach is dog-free in summer).

How to get there: A39 to Wadebridge. At Wadebridge roundabout, turn onto B3314, signed Polzeath. Turn left, signed St Minver Holiday Park & Golf Club. Turn right, signed St Moritz Hotel. Continue through the village of Trebetherick. On entering Polzeath, site is on the left, part way down the hill. NOTE: Ignore signs for Polzeath once on the B3314 and follow directions as above; other roads are extremely narrow in places and large 'vans could get stuck. Entrance to the site is tight, and on a steep hill.

Food & drink: The fully licensed Cracking Crab Beach Café next to the campsite has great food and location; it receives rave reviews for both its seafood and locally-sourced steaks. Breakfasts, lunchtime snacks and hearty dinners, including barbecues.

Nearby attractions: The beach – simple.

Alternative campsite: South Winds Camping and Caravanning (www.polzeathcamping.co.uk, tel.: 01208 863267). Run by the same owners, the site is on a hill half a mile out of Polzeath with great sea views.

Top: The beach at Polzeath, viewed from Tristram
Bottom Left: VW campervan pitched at Tristram
Bottom Right: Young surfers ready for the waves

Beacon Cottage Farm
Cornwall

The Cornish (or Celtic) name for the village of St Agnes is 'Bryanick'; it means 'a pointed hill' and refers to St Agnes Beacon, a prominent landmark to the west, and a giant of a hill 192 metres by comparison to the relatively flat terrain in the area.

Sheltering under the gaze of the hill is Beacon Cottage Farm Touring Park. It's within the walls of a traditional working farm and is allegedly the oldest campsite in Cornwall, set up over 75 years ago by Jane Sawle's grandfather. Jane runs the campsite now and her son looks after the cattle in the surrounding pastures.

Camping at Beacon Cottage is rather like camping in someone's garden. The flowers are out of this world and make a colourful, informal setting otherwise not found on large commercial sites. With the traditional farmhouse, oozing Cornish character, as the central point, there are six small paddocks separated by hedges, walls and flower beds, each one uniquely landscaped in the most natural of ways. There's the 'Top Paddock', secluded in the farthest corner from the house; 'Kate's Paddock', private and sheltered by a bank of primroses and bluebells in spring; the 'Orchard' and the 'Lawn' paddocks, where chickens are free to roam and provide campers with a fresh supply of breakfast material; and 'Bowland' and 'Goose Field', two slightly larger fields, still enclosed by lichen-covered stone walls, that look out over the remaining pastures and the most magnificent views of the north Cornish coastline.

When I first visited Beacon Cottage Farm with my family, the sun shone brilliantly, turning the sea to a peacock-blue with such depth of colour that a painter would have wept if they'd forgotten a brush. On our second visit a sea mist enveloped the headland so severely only a foot's length in front of you was visible. We opted for a walk on both occasions. The narrow lane just in front of

Above: The stunning view from the campsite

the campsite was, as usual, deserted and we could wander unhindered. Daffodils iced the walls, iridescent in the sunshine; harebells filled the roadside and violets punctuated the ivy-carpetted walls. The silence was magical, a trickle from the preceding rain was the only sound in the air, coupled with dusk birdsong.

There are plenty of opportunities to go for either a late evening stroll or a mammoth expeditionary hike. A footpath from the back of the campsite takes you to the Beacon, where views transport you to St Ives in the south-west and Newquay in the north-east, and all at the same time on a clear day. The fields are filled with daffodils in spring, a sight that cheers up the area on a dull day when summer hasn't quite made it. In front of Beacon Cottage Farm you can walk the view of the campsite, with paths that criss-cross the heather-matted heathland like a toddler's scribble, and the South West Coast Path follows along the very edge of the cliff top. The surrounding area has been designated a World Heritage Site for its historical connections with the world of mining; Wheal Coates, one such mine, stands magnificently against the cliff top, its chimney appearing to plummet into the frothing sea below.

While the campsite is tantalizingly close to the sea – a matter of yards – there's no access down the steep and craggy cliffs, against which the ocean crashes in a fearful rage. To appreciate the calmer, gentler waters, you need to make the ten-minute walk around the coastline to Chapel Porth beach, where swimmers, surfers and sun-loving beach babes unite on the sand. There are good times to be had here for families, too, with a series of caves and shallow rock pools to explore.

The village of St Agnes is 1½ miles from the site, either by road or on foot across the fields. Here you can stock up on provisions and search for a cream tea. The fish shop serves fresh specimens from the ocean; there's a first-class butchers selling handmade sausages and The Bakery sells a good old pasty made to a local recipe.

Legend has it that St Agnes has its very own giant, Bolster, who fell into the sea chasing an unrequited love; the blood-stained cave at nearby Chapel Porth is one mystery for the explorers in the family to solve. Beacon Cottage Farm, just round the corner, may be a small site, but it's a giant in terms of beauty and location.

Beacon Cottage Farm Touring Park

Beacon Drive, St Agnes, Cornwall, TR5 0NU

01872 552347

www.beaconcottagefarmholidays.co.uk

jane@beaconcottagefarmholidays.co.uk

Opening times: March to October

Facilities: 60 pitches, hook-ups, free hot showers, toilets in clean building, family room with shower, toilet, baby bath and changing area, dishwashing, laundry, chemical toilet disposal point, play area, dog walk, small shop, gas exchange. Dogs welcome.

How to get there: From A30, turn onto B3277, signed St Agnes. At mini-roundabout approaching St Agnes, turn left, signed Chapel Porth. Continue for 2 miles over crossroads and round a right-angled bend. Site is on the right. Last 2 miles are narrow.

Food & drink: Presingoll Farm (www.presingollfarm.co.uk, tel.: 01872 552333) sells its own organic meat. The owners also run the St Agnes Veg Shop, selling fresh, seasonal produce, most grown within a 15-mile radius of St Agnes. Look out for the Cornish pasties at the village bakery too. And there's a particularly fine beach cafe at Chapel Porth.

Nearby attractions: St Ives, with the Tate Gallery, makes a good day out 20 miles away. Or hop on a ½-hour flight from Newquay for a day trip to the Scilly Isles with beaches that seem tropical (www.visitislesofscilly.com), a unique day to remember.

Alternative campsite: Presingoll Farm (www.presingollfarm.co.uk, tel.: 01872 552333). Close to St Agnes on the B3277, a quiet farm site but without the coastal views.

Top: Beacon Cottage Farm
Bottom Left: Chickens roaming the grounds
Bottom Right: Daffodils growing atop a wall at Beacon Cottage Farm

Treloan Coastal Holidays
Cornwall

To find a campsite in Cornwall that's open out of the summer season is rare indeed; to find one right on the coast is like searching for a hen with teeth. Which is what makes Treloan campsite almost unique – it's in Cornwall, by the sea and it's open all year round. A good job, too, as it would be scandalous to save the incredible views for a few short months, denying access to a paling winter sun flashing over the bay when virtually the rest of Cornish camping has shut down.

Debs and her family bought the site in 2007, when it was a pitiful, run-down affair that needed lots of love. They gave it bucketloads and, with a Trojan-like work schedule, quickly brought the site up to speed, replacing old facilities for new. The amenity buildings are not five-star but neither are they great big ugly blocks to spoil the site; it's all totally adequate and clean with child-size facilities added, including a low-down washing-up sink – so, parents, it's time for a glass of wine unless you fear for your plastic plates.

Everything about Treloan oozes individuality and lots of thought about what visitors might like. As if the views overlooking Gerrans Bay were not enough (and they would be), Debs has a campsite full of community spirit, with gentle activities for all. If this conjures up images of giant holiday parks, rest assured – this is different. It's about much more laid-back – almost horizontal – wholesome eco art-based activities that stir the soul and kick-start the imagination. A large,

communal campfire set up in the 'Eco field', one down from the touring area, burns into the evening, around which storytellers spin a yarn and musicians strike up a tune. If you can play an instrument well enough so other visitors don't run for the exit, take it with you. Artists in residence stay on site from time to time to help out with brushing the magnificent views onto canvas and running workshops. 'Wild food' walks give visitors the opportunity to see the countryside with a

Above: Views from the campsite

different eye, as they learn to forage for tasty goodies in the hedgerows. And children help out with egg collecting and feeding duties with the menagerie of chickens, rabbits, pigs, goats – and a ferret. They can help in the 'Edible Corner' too, where the campsite veg and soft fruits are lovingly tended, compassionately learning about the food they eat; and eat you can with fresh produce from the campsite allotment for sale. Environmentally conscious camping is at the heart of the campsite.

If all this sounds a bit too collective and you'd prefer a few hours of privacy conversing with your own thoughts, then there are individual braziers for hire and barbecues by your 'van are allowed (off the grass) too.

Enough unique qualities? Nope, not on your nelly. Aside from the seven mobile homes available for hire, visitors can also stay in the Honeycomb Snug or the Yurt. Sleeping two, either is perfect for a romantic stay – possibly even a honeymoon, as the campsite can also provide a wedding field to exchange rings and celebrate the nuptials while gazing out to sea. Debs can arrange the marquee and the catering if required, and you can book the entire site for wedding guests, making it the tiniest of steps back to the accommodation when the Champagne stops flowing.

The 64 pitches on the campsite make the most of the sea views, each one with lots of space. A footpath takes bathers the 300 metres to the beach, which connects up with the South West Coast Path. This National Trail runs along to the lively village of Portscatho, which is popular with the sailing fraternity because of its harbour. On the top of the hill, and a three-minute walk from the campsite, is Gerrans, the quieter of the two villages. The whole of the Roseland Peninsula is walking heaven, with plentiful footpaths, quiet lanes and a wealth of flora and fauna. At the tip of the peninsula you can catch a ferry to the fishing village of St Mawes, saving the trip by car around the Percuil river estuary.

Treloan is unique, maybe, and magical, definitely.

Treloan Coastal Holidays

Treloan Lane, Gerrans, Portscatho, Cornwall,
TR2 5EF

01872 580989

www.treloancoastalholidays.co.uk

info@treloancoastalholidays.co.uk

Opening times: Open all year

Facilities: 64 pitches, hook-ups, free hot showers, toilets, dishwashing, seven mobile homes and a yurt for hire, wedding field for hire, braziers for hire, field for ball games, eco/art activities and workshops. Dogs welcome.

How to get there: From A390 St Austell to Truro road, turn onto A3078, signed St Mawes, half a mile past Trewithian, turn left, signed Gerrans. In village centre, between the church and The Royal Standard pub, turn into Treloan Lane. Site is 300 yards farther on the left.

Food & drink: The Hidden Hut (www.hiddenhut.co.uk) on Porthcurnick Beach, 1/2 mile from the campsite. It's a very popular and trendy beach cafe serving amazing food and drink, including notable open-air feast nights that, alone, are worthy of a stay at Treloan.

Nearby attractions: Trelissick Garden (NT), a 30-acre colour palette, is 5 miles away via the King Harry ferry. Hire a wooden sailing boat for the day and explore Falmouth Bay and the creeks (www.mylorboathire.co.uk).

Alternative campsite: Trethem Mill (www.trethem.com, tel.: 01872 580504). Three miles from Treloan Coastal Holidays off the A3078 St Mawes road, a quiet site with lots of pitches.

Top: A busy summer at Treloan Coastal Holidays
Bottom Left: Views from Treloan Coastal Holidays
Bottom Right: Blackberries ripening beside the South West Coast Path, accessed from the campsite

Treveague Farm
Cornwall

If there's ever a place to learn about nature and the environment, Treveague Farm is right up there with the best. Just talk to Steve and Myra, the owners, and they'll enlighten visitors with all sorts of anecdotes about the natural world. Like all the best campsites, Treveague farm is constantly evolving and improving, while at its heart it maintains traditional values.

Above: Treveague Farm is a working sheep farm

Since buying the place in 2001, Steve and Myra have converted 200 acres of farmland to organic status, built four beautiful stone holiday cottages, rebuilt the amenity block on the campsite for visitors to have a far more relaxing shower and upgraded many of the facilities. That's no mean feat when you're also looking after the land using much more labour-intensive farming methods, caring for a herd of cattle, a flock of sheep and some pigs (marketing the produce to local restaurants) – not to mention attending to the needs of expectant campsite visitors hell-bent on having a good time.

So, to make things a little easier, Steve and Myra like to include guests in life around the farm, encouraging them to look after the pigs and feed the spring lambs. They also like visitors to find out what freshly prepared food, direct from the farm, tastes like, and for you to recycle everything you can while on the farm (or not to waste it in the first place). But perhaps the most exciting of all their innovations is the wildlife hide in the woods that Steve has made.

In a secluded corner of the farm, passing mind-blowing views of the sea, guests can sit – ever so still and silently – in the hide, peeking out of the little slit windows, to watch the birds feeding and the dragonflies hovering over the natural spring-fed pond. After dark, badgers and foxes come out to play right in front of your noses, their actions and movements caught on wide-screen monitors. With night-vision cameras and recording facilities in the hide, you can make your own wildlife film to take home, a unique memory of a great holiday. There's the opportunity for nature walks around the area as well, so one can fully appreciate their surroundings.

The campsite takes over a field in the centre of the farm. With room for 40 touring 'vans, it has lovely views of the sea in opposite directions, looking towards Veryan Bay and the Roseland Peninsula one way and Gorran Haven the other. Should children find the time in between feeding the animals and nature walks, there's

Right: The views to the sea from Treveague Farm

a pretty nifty timber adventure fort on which they can become knights, cavaliers and rescued princesses for an hour or two.

The campsite shop offers a few basics as well as tasty organic treats from the farm, with bread and cakes ordered in fresh from the baker. The Secret Garden eatery, tucked into another corner of the site, does breakfast, coffee and cake and evening meals, serving the farm's produce whenever possible and otherwise locally-sourced. Don't expect bland pub-grub; these are taste sensations like slow-cooked lamb reared on the farm. Guests supply their own wine.

With such fine views tempting campers down to the rolling surf, it would be cruel to find no way of reaching it. Fortunately, there are three sandy beaches within 10 to 25 minutes' walk of the campsite, across lovely open farmland and down little Cornish lanes, the roadsides brimming with wild flowers.

To experience flowers in a more formal setting and to carry on the nature studies, the Lost Gardens of Heligan are just 3 miles from the campsite. There is unimaginable beauty in the gardens, which have been restored from initial findings that came to light after the devastating storm of 1990. You should set aside several hours to soak up the scents and drown your eyes with colour in the various intermingling gardens with secret connecting paths. It's impossible not to be overcome by the towering rhododendrons that fill the skyline with pink or feel quite so insignificant against the gargantuan specimens of the jungle.

At Treveague Steve and Myra don't like too many rules, so they've created just one – respect. Respect for their farm, respect for nature and respect for fellow campers. And our respect to Steve and Myra for inviting campers onto their beautiful farm.

Treveague Farm Campsite

Gorran, St Austell, Cornwall, PL26 6NY

01726 842295

www.treveaguefarm.co.uk

info@treveaguefarm.co.uk

Opening times: April to September

Facilities: 40 pitches, hook-ups, hot showers (tokens), toilets, chemical toilet disposal point, dishwashing, laundry, recycling facilities, play area, small shop and bottled gas, cafe/restaurant, nature hide and walks. Dogs welcome (on leads).

How to get there: From A390 at St Austell, turn onto B3273 for Mevagissey. After climbing from Pentewan, turn right, signed the Lost Gardens of Heligan. Pass the gardens and continue towards Gorran. In 3 miles (before Gorran), fork right, signed for Seaview International & Treveague Farm. At T-junction turn left and then almost immediately right, signed Treveague Farm. The site entrance is directly ahead of you as the road bends round to the right. The last 2 miles are narrow, but quiet.

Food & drink: The Secret Garden Eatery on site. For fantastic food to prepare in your 'van, Lobbs Farm Shop (www.lobbsfarmshop.com, tel.: 01726 844411), in the grounds of the Lost Gardens of Heligan, has a butchers and deli counter and a wide range of local produce, including Cornish wines and beers, jams and chocolate, plus locally grown seasonal fruit and vegetables.

Alternative campsite: Seaview International (www.seaviewinternational.com, tel.: 01726 843725). Large, award-winning holiday park with static and touring areas and all the facilities associated with a big site. Sea views from the touring area too.

Top: Cattle graze the land at Treveague Farm
Bottom Left: The Lost Gardens of Heligan
Bottom Right: The play area at Treveague Farm

Pentewan Sands
Cornwall

You could be forgiven for dismissing Pentewan as one of those places that, on first glance, seems too big and impersonal. Driving past, it's only row upon row of statics that first catch your eye; there's no knowing what lies beyond. Then, turning a bend in the road, you climb up a steep hill out of Pentewan towards Mevagissey and you will be awestruck by what you see: one huge, grassy touring park and one huge silver-sanded private beach, the exclusive use given over to guests of the park.

The 32-acre site has a whopping 126 mobile homes and 534 touring pitches, a mixture of hook-ups and non-electric, and in the weeks when the little darlings are on their summer holidays it's more akin to a festival campsite than a quiet retreat. But its location still wins over, the lure of a beach a few paces away. The park is also tastefully modest in the style of building, and any entertainments that are laid on are all contained in one area, which you can take or leave. The beach is the draw and most will be on it from sunrise until sunset.

To put things in perspective, the park lies in a river valley betwixt the road from St Austell to Mevagissey and the deep blue sea. It's a B-road that, once you're on site, is unnoticeable and doesn't keep you awake at night. Lining the site from the road are the mobile homes, not the prettiest to look at but pleasant and modern inside; the park does at least keep their fleet of mobile homes up to date with the very latest models. The remainder of the park is taken up with grass pitches connected by tarmac roads. They're split into sections, with the premier pitches, right at the front of the site next to the beach, costing the most. On either side, beautiful rugged cliffs rise up, drawing the eye along the coastline. The beach, sheltered in its own bay, has some of the softest sand in Cornwall and has been given the thumbs up by the Marine Conservation Society for its cleanliness. In peak season swimmers are separated from the boat-launching slipway – yes, you can bring your own boat – and waterski pick-up area (lessons are provided by the site and diving tuition is also available).

Above: Pitches at Pentewan Sands

If squidging sand between the toes doesn't appeal, or the prospect of trying to get it out of the 'van for the rest of the season, there are two heated outdoor swimming pools (grown-ups and toddlers) in the 'entertainment' area, along with a tennis court, playground, the Cornish-themed Jolly Roger pub and stylish, chic Seahorse Restaurant, and a shop more akin in style and size to that on a continental campsite, where you can buy delicious fresh bread and croissants in the morning along with surfing gear and a new bathing outfit. If you can't prise yourself away from the beach, the Hubbox should keep you replenished with a fresh-made burger and beer.

Out of peak season the site is spectacular, with lots of space and a beach virtually to yourself, except for the odd lonesome fisherman. A cycle trail follows the line of the adjacent road (with bike hire available on site) and the South West Coastal Path runs right around the site and up to the cliffs towards Mevagissey and Black Head.

Round and about, Mevagissey is the place to go for fish and chips by the sea while watching all the fishing boats bouncing up and down in the water, the nets cast aside on the harbour wall ready for the next big catch. It's only a couple of miles from the site, easily reached along the coast path or by bike – and motorhomes can stop in the privately owned car park at the entrance to the village, just before the narrow warren of streets begin. To sample Britain's traditional dish twice over, catch the ferry from Mevagissey to Fowey, another spectacularly beautiful (and spectacularly steep) Cornish fishing village on the other side of St Austell Bay, tucked up into the estuary of the River Fowey; sometimes there's even the odd dolphin or two moseying about the bay.

Approximately 10 miles from Pentewan is the Eden Project, and closer still, within cycling distance if you don't mind hills, are the Lost Gardens of Heligan. For a taste of Cornish heritage, the China Clay Country Park near St Austell explains the important role that the china clay industry played in the life of the region; set in the grounds of two former Victorian mines, 26 acres of woodland and nature trails now cover the working area and an interactive museum tells the story.

But with so much sand, sea and suncream at Pentewan, the best stories will be those told around the family table in years to come of camping by the beach.

Pentewan Sands Holiday Park

Pentewan, Cornwall, PL26 6BT

01726 843485

www.pentewan.co.uk

info@pentewan.co.uk

Opening times: March to end of October

Facilities: 534 touring pitches with and without hook-ups, static caravans for hire, hot showers, toilets, chemical toilet disposal points, dishwashing, laundry, Cornish-themed pub, two restaurants, takeaway, large shop, swimming pools, tennis court, private beach, play area, cycle hire, boat launch, certified watersports training centre with tuition, children's club in high season, wi-fi. Dogs welcome.

How to get there: From A390 at St Austell, turn onto B3273, signed Mevagissey. Pentewan Sands is 4 miles on the left from the A390/B3273 roundabout.

Food & drink: Fish and chips in Mevagissey do the business, and there are lots to choose from around the harbour. Otherwise, Pentewan Sands' own restaurants and pub all use locally-produced Cornish ingredients and provide plenty of choice.

Nearby attractions: Cornwall's only city, Truro, is 18 miles from Pentewan. Bodmin Moor provides a change in scenery to the beach for some hillside walking.

Alternative campsite: Treveague Farm (*see* page 206, www.treveaguefarm.co.uk, tel.: 01726 842295) is 5 miles from Pentewan, with sea views.

Top Left: The private beach at Pentewan Sands
Top Right: The play area at Pentewan Sands
Bottom: Mevagissey Harbour

Index

Alpine Grove Woodland Park 176–8
Austwick, N. Yorkshire 40–3

Bakewell Camping and Caravanning Club Site 72–5
Banbury, Oxfordshire 84–7
Bank House Farm 76–9
Beacon Cottage Farm Touring Park 198–201
Berkshire 136–43
Berrynarbor, North Devon 186–9
Bolberry House Farm 182–5
Borrowdale Caravan Club Site 20–3
Burrowhayes Farm 172–5

Cambridgeshire 128–31
Castlerigg Farm Camping and Caravan Site 12–15
Castleton, Derbyshire 68–71
Chard, Somerset 176–8
Chertsey Camping and Caravanning Club Site 144–7
Chine Farm Camping Site 156–9
Church Farm Organics 64–7
Church Stile Farm Holiday Park 16–19
Coniston, Cumbria 24–7
Coniston Park Coppice Caravan Club Site 24–7
Corfe Castle Camping and Caravanning Club Site 168–71
Cornwall 194–213
County Durham 48–55
Cumbria 12–27

Denny Wood Campsite 152–5
Derbyshire 68–75
Devon 182–93
Dorset 164–71
Dower House Touring Park, The 116–19

East Harling, Norfolk 116–19
Exmoor, Somerset 179–81

Finchale Abbey Caravan Park 48–51
Fir Tree Farm Caravan Park 84–7

Gloucestershire 104–7

Halse Farm 179–81
Haltwhistle Camping and Caravanning Club Site 60–3
Hampshire 152–5
Hartington, Staffordshire 76–9
Hayles Fruit Farm 104–7
Herefordshire 100–3
Hexham, Northumberland 56–9
Highside Farm 52–5
Horton, Dorset 164–7
Howgill Lodge 36–9
Huntingdon, Cambridgeshire 128–31
Hurley Riverside Park 136–9

Isle of Wight 156–9

Karrageen 182–5
Kent 148–51
Keswick, Cumbria 12–15, 20–3
Kielder Village Caravan and Campsite 56–9
Kingsbridge, South Devon 182–5
Knighton, Shropshire 92–5

Lincoln Farm Park 132–5
Lincolnshire 80–3
Lound House Farm 28–31
Ludlow, Shropshire 96–9
Lyndhurst, Hampshire 152–5

Marden, Kent 148–51
Marlborough, Wiltshire 160–3
Merseyside 64–7
Middleton-in-Teesdale, County Durham 52–5
Minehead, Somerset 172–5
Monaughty Poeth 92–5

Napps Touring Park 186–9
Norfolk 108–19

North Morte Farm Caravan and Camping Park 190–3
North Yorkshire 28–47
Northumberland 56–63

Oaklea CL 80–3
Orchard Campsite, The 120–3
Oxfordshire 132–5

Pentewan Sands Holiday Park 210–13
Portscatho, Cornwall 202–5
Postern Hill Caravan and Camping Site 160–3
Potter Heigham, Norfolk 112–15

Reading, Berkshire 140–3
Ripon, N. Yorkshire 32–5
Riverside Lakes 164–7
Rowlestone Court 100–3
Rowter Farm 68–71
Run Cottage Touring Park 124–7

St Agnes, Cornwall 198–201
St Austell, Cornwall 206–9
Sandringham Camping and Caravanning Club Site 108–11
Seascale, Cumbria 16–19
Shropshire 92–9
Skipton, N. Yorkshire 36–9
Sleningford Watermill 32–5
Somerset 172–81
Staffordshire 76–9
Stratford Touring Park 88–91
Suffolk 120–7
Surrey 144–7
Swaledale, N. Yorkshire 44–7

Tanner Farm Park 148–51
Treloan Coastal Holidays 202–5
Treveague Farm Campsite 206–9
Tristram Camping Park 194–7

Usha Gap Caravans and Camping 44–7

Ventnor, Isle of Wight 156–9

Wadebridge, Cornwall 194–7
Wareham, Dorset 168–71
Warwickshire 84–91
Waterclose Meadows Campsite 128–31
Wellington Country Park 140–3
Wharfedale, N. Yorkshire 36–9
Whitby, N. Yorkshire 28–31
Whitcliffe Campsite 96–9
Wickham Market, Suffolk 120–3
Willowcroft Camping and Caravan Park 112–15
Wiltshire 160–3
Winchcombe, Gloucestershire 104–7
Wirral, Merseyside 64–7
Witney, Oxfordshire 132–5
Woodbridge, Suffolk 124–7
Woodend Farm 40–3
Woodhall Spa, Lincolnshire 80–3
Woolacombe, North Devon 190–3

Published 2017—IMM Lifestyle Books
www.IMMLifestyleBooks.com

IMM Lifestyle Books are distributed in the UK by Grantham Book Service,
Trent Road, Grantham, Lincolnshire, NG31 7XQ.

In North America, IMM Lifestyle Books are distributed by
Fox Chapel Publishing, 1970 Broad Street, East Petersburg, PA 17520,
www.FoxChapelPublishing.com

ISBN 978-1-5048-0071-6

Printed in Singapore
10 9 8 7 6 5 4 3 2 1

The author and publisher have made every effort to ensure that all
information given in this book is accurate, but they cannot accept liability
for any resulting injury or loss or damage to either property or person,
whether direct or consequential and howsoever arising.